COSTLY GRACE

90-DAY DEVOTIONAL

A companion to
COSTLY GRACE
A Contemporary View of
Bonhoeffer's
The Cost of Discipleship

JON WALKER

LEAFWOOD
PUBLISHERS

COSTLY GRACE 90-DAY DEVOTIONAL

L E A F W O O D
P U B L I S H E R S

Copyright 2010 by Jon Walker

ISBN 978-0-89112-677-5
LCCN 2010034713

Printed in the United States of America

LIBRARY OF CONGRESS CATALOGING-IN-PUBLICATION DATA
Walker, Jon, 1958-
 Costly grace 90-day devotional : a contemporary view of Bonhoeffer's The cost of discipleship / Jon Walker.
   p. cm.
 ISBN 978-0-89112-677-5
 1. Bonhoeffer, Dietrich, 1906-1945. Nachfolge. 2. Grace (Theology)--Meditations. I. Title.
 BT380.B6593W34 2010
 234--dc22
                                                        2010034713

Cover and interior text design by Thinkpen Design, Inc

Published in association with Rosenbaum & Associates Literary Agency, Brentwood, Tennessee.

Leafwood Publishers is an imprint of
Abilene Christian University Press
1626 Campus Court
Abilene, Texas 79601
1-877-816-4455
www.leafwoodpublishers.com

COSTLY GRACE

90-DAY DEVOTIONAL

Dedication

To Mark Kelly

"There is a friend who sticks closer than a brother."
—Proverbs 18:24

TABLE OF CONTENTS

ACKNOWLEDGMENTS

It is impossible to write a book without admitting, like Tennyson, "I am part of all that I have met." That being the case, it is beyond my abilities to thank everyone who helped me while writing this devotional, but I do want to mention: Steve Pettit and Rick Warren have both mentored me in their own ways, and their influence permeates this text. My thanks also to Susan Goetz, Mark Kelly, Lori Hensley, Matt Tullos, Grace Guthrie, Paul Carlisle, Dan Stone, Kathy Chapman Sharp, Donna Stetzer, Doug Hart, Bucky Rosenbaum, Gary Myers, Leonard Allen, Terry Whaley, Jordan Camenker, Kim Glaner, Sam Butler, Tobin Perry, Robert Supernor, Ryan Carson, Kristine Noelle, and Laura Vest, whose gift of Pumpkin, the cuddling cockapoo, quite honestly saved my life.

INTRODUCTION

Dietrich Bonheoffer believed that, when we follow Jesus, we are called to an extraordinary life, but one full of risks. He taught that Jesus pushes us into places where we must make a choice for him: will we follow after him or will we stay where we are?

Bonhoeffer's authenticity appeals to me. He walked steadily toward an uncompromising faith in Jesus, and he did it in the difficult and dangerous years when the Nazi regime ruled Germany. Bonhoeffer saw others in the church compromising their faith in the face of Hitler, and so he called Christians to follow Jesus no matter where he leads. Ultimately, this led Bonhoeffer to a hang-man's noose, his death ordered by Hitler just a few weeks before Germany's surrender.

Bonhoeffer's uncompromising trust in Jesus speaks across the generations; his teaching is as relevant today as it was in 1937 when *The Cost of Discipleship* was first published. In *Costly Grace: A Contemporary View of Bonhoeffer's The Cost of Discipleship*,, I tried to make Bonhoeffer's teaching—where every sentence is ripe with deep, spiritual insight—accessible to the average reader.

But honestly, my prayer is that *Costly Grace* will be more to you than just a resource that teaches you about Jesus or about Dietrich Bonhoeffer's teachings. My prayer is that, after reading the book, you will know Jesus and have an ever developing desire to know him more.

To that end, there are some key concepts to keep in mind as you read these devotionals:

- We get to know Jesus by following Jesus. We want to hear from him, the Word of God. We want to follow Christ and Christ alone, not some formula or image of what we think Christianity should be.
- We're engaged in a relationship, not a religion. The most significant question we must always ask is "who?" Questions of "how" or "why" are secondary, and we must be cautious that they do not take priority over "who," "how," and "why" questions tend to focus us on a system, on rituals, on religion; "who" brings us back to the relationship.
- When we follow Jesus, his life flows through us— from God to Jesus to us to others. When we remain self-centered, we interrupt the flow. But this flow also means that Jesus fills us completely; we cannot compartmentalize the life of Christ within us or segment it to parts of our existence. When we follow Jesus, we are engaged in what theologians call sanctification, which, essentially, could be described as Christ eliminating the blockages in our life that keep his life from flowing into every area of our being.

- We learn to trust Jesus through our obedience to Jesus. Jesus calls; we come. Jesus commands; we obey. We want it to be: Jesus calls; we decide if we'll come after we determine if it works for us. Jesus commands; we obey after he explains everything to us and lets us decide if it is convenient for us. The only way to develop faith is to reverse this process, to obey the commands of Jesus and then, in our obedience, we see that Jesus is trustworthy. That is, we learn to trust him more.

- The key to deeper faith—to being a better Christian, so to speak—is not trying harder to be good, but trusting Jesus more. This is a critical concept and one where we stumble the most. Religion requires that we try harder; our relationship with Jesus requires us to *trust* more.

These concepts are at the core of this devotional. They form the backdrop for each day's devotional,

The ninety devotionals in this book are meant to be a companion to *Costly Grace*. They are drawn from the main book, but have been adapted and enhanced to bring out the devotional elements.

The devotional stands on its own for use by individuals or by a small group. It can be used simultaneously while reading *Costly Grace*, employing it like a supplemental lab to the classroom presentation of the main book. If you choose to use it for a small group study, you can find small group discussion guides at www.costlygracetoday.com.

You might also consider reading it after you've read *Costly Grace*, giving you ninety days to incorporate the cost of discipleship into your life. You will find materials related to that at www.costlygracetoday.com.

May you enter the rest of God, fully trusting in his promises to you, and may you follow Jesus faithfully through the narrow gate into the kingdom of heaven, where the Father rejoices because you are coming home to him.

Jon Walker

Jacob's Landing

August 2010

DAY 1

Christ and Christ Alone

What shall we say, then? Shall we go on sinning
so that grace may increase? By no means! We
have died to sin; how can we live in it any longer?

—ROMANS 6:1–2

"If they follow Jesus, men escape from the hard yoke
of their own laws, and submit to the kindly yoke
of Jesus Christ. But does this mean that we ignore
the seriousness of his commands? Far from it."

—DIETRICH BONHOEFFER

Most of us would like to live a life of extraordinary quality that is not only fulfilling but also carries significance beyond ourselves. It's most likely one of the reasons you became a Christian, and it is *exactly* the kind of life Jesus promises if we will follow him.

So, why isn't it happening? Why, instead of the abundant life, do so many of us end up living lives of *quiet desperation*? We go to church; we read the Bible; we pray; we try to be good people and to serve other people. Yet, for many of us, our life with Jesus doesn't seem to be much more than an add-on to our increasingly complex lives. We are over-stretched and now seem to be facing a tsunami of uncertainty in many areas that for so long have seemed relatively secure—our finances, our jobs, our homes, and even our fundamental safety.

So we try harder, work harder, pray harder, study harder, and try to figure out what we're doing wrong because that's what we think Jesus wants us to do. And, all the while, he keeps asking, in a sense, "Are you tired of this yet?"

"Worn out? Burned out on religion? Come to me. Get away with me and you'll recover your life. I'll show you how to take a real rest. Walk with me and work with me—watch how I do it. Learn the unforced rhythms of grace" (Matt. 11:28b-29 MSG).

Jesus calls us away from the hows and whys and whats into the rhythms of his grace, standing before us as the Son of God Incarnate, Jesus, God's Word in the flesh. The answer to our frustrations is "who," not "what" or "how."

The Word of God who stands before us is not a problem to be solved, but a person to know, and when we try to relate to him as a "how" or "what," we end up in the never-ending cycle of trying harder to fit into an equation that God never meant for us to solve.

Instead of trying harder, let's trust more.

DAY 2

Cheap Grace Justifies Sin, Not the Sinner

Then neither do I condemn you. . . .
Go now and leave your life of sin.

—JOHN 8:11

"Cheap grace is the preaching of forgiveness
without requiring repentance, baptism without
church discipline, Communion without confession,
absolution without personal confession."

—DIETRICH BONHOEFFER

By cheap grace, Bonhoeffer means the arrogant presumption that we can receive forgiveness for our sins, yet never abandon our lives to Jesus. We assume, since grace is free, there is no cost associated with the free gift.

The gift is free, but Jesus paid a bloody price to offer us the gift. The gift is free, but that doesn't mean there is no cost to following Jesus once we step into his grace.

Costly grace justifies the sinner—Go and sin no more. Cheap grace justifies the sin—Everything is forgiven, so you can stay as you are.

To assume that God's grace is nothing more than a way to "get out of jail free" undermines the kingly crown of thorns Jesus wore on the cross. We do not receive God's grace to make us feel better about ourselves while we live in this world; rather, God gives it in order for us to enter into the kingdom of heaven even as we live in this world.

Jesus rescued the woman caught in adultery from certain death, but his expectation was that her life would change immediately. To return to her old life would have mocked the very grace that Jesus gave that day. His expectation of a changed life is no different for us: "Go now and leave your life of sin."

DAY 3

Following the Real Jesus

You search the Scriptures because you believe they give
you eternal life. But the Scriptures point to me! Yet you
refuse to come to me so that I can give you this eternal life.

—JOHN 5:39–40 (NLT)

"What we want to know is not, what would this
or that man, or this or that Church, have of
us, but what Jesus Christ himself wants of us."

—DIETRICH BONHOEFFER

Being a disciple means we are inseparably bonded to Jesus: he is the curriculum we study; he is the Word we believe; and he is the Way we live.

The more intimate we become with Jesus, the more successful we will be at becoming like him.

This is why we're to preach and teach Christ and Christ alone. But Bonhoeffer says we're in danger of abandoning Christ in two ways, and both are as prevalent today as they were in Bonhoeffer's generation.

First, he says the church has reduced the Gospel to a set of burdensome rules, the antithesis of the easy yoke we should find in Jesus. We've loaded the Gospel down with so many extra-biblical rules and regulations—a real Christian ought to, has to, must do—that it is difficult for anyone to find the real Jesus, let alone make a clear and conscious decision to follow Christ.

Second, he says we've wrapped the Gospel in false hopes and consolations, using the doctrine of grace as an excuse for shallow discipleship and an acceptance of sin. Grace is meant to justify the sinner; yet, we use it to justify our sins. In other words, we've taken "I am a sinner saved by grace" and turned it into "I can sin because of grace."

In either case (whether we embrace a burdensome religion or a presumptive attitude toward grace), we end up practicing a religion far removed from the intimate relationship God requires that we have with Jesus Christ.

Where do you fall in this spectrum? Burdensome religion? Presumptive attitude? Intimate relationship with the son of God?

DAY 4

Denying the Incarnation

[He] took upon him the form of a servant, and was made in the likeness of men: And being found in fashion as a man, humbled himself, and became obedience unto death, even the death of the cross.

—PHILIPPIANS 2:7B–8 (KJV)

"Cheap grace is grace without discipleship, grace without the cross, grace without Jesus Christ, living and incarnate."

—DIETRICH BONHOEFFER

Did Jesus die so we could follow a doctrine? Did he suffer a cruel and bloody crucifixion to give us a code of conduct?

Did he give up all he had, take on the nature of a servant, and walk through Palestine as a human being so we could give an intellectual assent to the grace he freely gives?

Did he humble himself and walk the path of obedience all the way to death so we could live in disobedience to him?

When the forgiveness of sin is proclaimed as a general truth and the love of God taught as a concept, we depersonalize the Incarnation, yet it can't be anything but personal: the God of the universe launching a rescue mission for you, his beloved creation, at the expense of Jesus, his one and only son.

The Incarnation is personal; the call of Jesus is personal; and the cost of grace is personal. We are called to come face-to-face with Jesus so that we can come to know him as completely as he knows us. "Now we see but a poor reflection as in a mirror; then we shall see face to face. Now I know in part; then I shall know fully, even as I am fully known" (1 Cor. 13:12).

Why do you think Jesus died for you? What do you think he expects from you?

DAY 5

Why Is Grace Costly If It Is a Free Gift from God?

I would like to learn just one thing from you: Did you receive the Spirit by observing the law, or by believing what you heard?

—Galatians 3:2

"[Jesus] held that the only way to safeguard the gospel of forgiveness was by preaching repentance."

—Dietrich Bonhoeffer

Grace is a sanctuary surrounded by sin and God's corresponding law. Outside the sanctuary, the law must destroy sin. Outside the sanctuary, the law demands perfection. No matter how good you are, if you slip just once, you have violated the law. You have sinned. Outside the sanctuary of grace, the wages of sin is death.

When you step into the sanctuary of grace, you are no longer pursued by the law. You are safe within the righteousness of Christ. You are free to live boldly, free of the fear that you might sin.

But that doesn't mean that the law no longer functions. The law continues its work outside the sanctuary. You can enter the sanctuary of grace for free; however, you cannot bring anything into the sanctuary with you. You must leave everything behind and begin a new way of living within the sanctuary of God's grace.

Cheap grace assumes you can live in God's sanctuary away from the law while remaining independent of God's desires:

> You used to live in sin, just like the rest of the world, obeying the devil—the commander of the powers in the unseen world. He is the spirit at work in the hearts of those who refuse to obey God. All of us used to live that way, following the passionate desires and inclinations of our sinful nature. By our very nature we were subject to God's anger, just like everyone else.
>
> But God is so rich in mercy, and he loved us so much, that even though we were dead because of our sins, he gave us life when he raised Christ from the dead. (It is only by God's grace that you have been saved!) (Eph. 2:1–5 nlt)

DAY 6

Nothing Remains the Same

For in Christ all the fullness of the Deity lives in bodily form,
and you have been given fullness in Christ,
who is the head over every power and authority.

—COLOSSIANS 2:9–10

"Costly grace is the treasure hidden in the field; for the
sake of it a man will gladly go and sell all that he has."

—DIETRICH BONHOEFFER

God plants this love inside us, and it grows healthy in
the soil of abandonment. We abandon our rights,
our judgments, our opinions, and our schemes. Jesus is
uncompromising in his abandonment of the privileges of
his position as the only begotten son, and he expects no
less from us when it comes to abandoning anything that
sets us in rebellion to the Father.

Like the man who found treasure hidden in a field,
he sells everything he has in order to buy the field. He
holds back nothing because he knows the treasure is
worth more than anything he has. Abandonment means

realizing that following Jesus is worth everything we have and so holding nothing back.

Costly grace requires that we come to the end of ourselves, that we abandon our current lives in order to begin new lives with Jesus. Costly grace means, "I have been crucified with Christ and I no longer live, but Christ lives in me. The life I live in the body, I live by faith in the Son of God, who loved me and gave himself for me" (Gal. 2:20).

Costly grace means we refuse to "set aside the grace of God" for the lesser things of this world (Gal. 2:21).

Abandonment is possible because you have Jesus within, helping you to love and obey. Let him lead you to that place where your heart begins to beat so closely with God's that it's difficult to distinguish between the two.

Love God, and in the intimacy of that love, obey his heart.

DAY 7

Jesus Defines My Life

Obedience is thicker than blood. The person who obeys my
heavenly Father's will is my brother and sister and mother.
—Matthew 12:50 (msg)

"When we are called to follow Christ, we are
summoned to an exclusive attachment to his person."
—Dietrich Bonhoeffer

Paul says that grace is a mystery, hard to explain, but
that perhaps we catch a glimpse of it in marriage
(Eph. 5:31–32). When you marry, you leave your old life
behind and begin a new life that is other-centered. You
become one with another and all of your relationships are
changed because you now live within this marriage.

It is expected that you will throw away the proverbial
little black book of lists the people you have been dating
or wanted to date. It is expected that you will relate to the
opposite sex in a different way. You are no longer single;
you are married. You belong to another; in truth, you are
joined to the other. You are one with the other.

You will also relate differently with your same gender friends. It is expected that you won't just take off and do what you want. You are one with another. You communicate and coordinate together.

This is what our relationship with Jesus is meant to be like. We are in union with him. Our oneness with him is similar to that of a husband and wife. We cannot relate to other people in the same way we did before we became joined with Jesus.

Even the way you relate to your mother, father, sister, or brother must change, which is why Jesus says, "If anyone comes to me and does not hate his father and mother, his wife and children, his brothers and sisters—yes, even his own life—cannot be my disciple" (Luke 14:26).

We may think we can compartmentalize our relationships, but the reality is we cannot relate to anyone as if we are separated from Jesus.

You can't say, "Jesus is part of my life" or "Jesus is important to my life." You should now say, "Jesus defines my life." Who does define your life? If not Jesus, then talk honestly to God about why?

DAY 8

The Paradox of Choice

And his commands are not burdensome . . . .

—1 JOHN 5:3

"When Jesus brings us to a choice, the choice itself is easy, it is our decision that is hard because to follow Jesus means to abandon the life of apparent convenience."

—DIETRICH BONHOEFFER

As we follow Jesus down the hard path through the narrow gate into the kingdom of heaven, we find he consistently moves us toward a choice—and then he demands we make the choice. Will you follow him into the kingdom of heaven, or will you remain a citizen of this world?

You can remain in the kingdom of this world, but then you are not his disciple. Bonhoeffer says, "It is the paradox of choice. When we live as a citizen of this world we seek easy choices that lead to an easy life. However, when Jesus brings us to a choice, the choice itself is easy, it is our decision that is hard because to follow Jesus means to abandon the life of apparent convenience."

Bonhoeffer says the commands of Jesus free us from the chains of our own religious traditions. By submitting to Jesus wholeheartedly, we are free to be who we were created to be as we enjoy fellowship with Jesus.

Jesus is not arbitrary or naive in his rule. He knows the realities of this life, but he also knows the realities of eternity. His eye is on the endgame. He knows there will be a judgment for those outside his grace, and so he approaches this world with a different point of view. Even on the cross, his prayer was for forgiveness and not vengeance, and that is a perspective we must learn as we move from thinking like fallen beings to thinking like citizens in the kingdom of heaven.

We may not understand all Jesus does, and that scares us, but that is also where faith emerges. It is at this critical junction between fear and faith that we can see the cost of discipleship clearly—and so Jesus pushes us constantly to this place of choice, where we follow in faith or pull back in fear.

Think about your choices. What do they say about your relationship with Jesus?

DAY 9

Abandon All or Abandon Jesus

Walk with me and work with me—watch how I do it.
Learn the unforced rhythms of grace. I won't lay anything
heavy or ill-fitting on you. Keep company with me and
you'll learn to live freely and lightly.

—Matthew 11:29–30 (MSG)

"There is only one way of believing on
Jesus Christ, and that is by leaving all and
going with the incarnate Son of God."

—Dietrich Bonhoeffer

Jesus calls us to a level of intimacy that can only be sustained by his constant presence in our lives. He won't allow us to pretend Christianity is an add-on philosophy to the life we've mapped out for ourselves. To follow Jesus means we abandon all or we abandon Jesus.

This includes abandoning any ideas about discipleship that don't include an intimate relationship with Jesus. Discipleship without Jesus is not discipleship. Bonhoeffer notes we may get excited about an abstract, intellectual discipleship and even try to put it into practice. But an idea is not a personal relationship; we can never follow an idea in intimate, personal obedience.

"Christianity without the living Christ is inevitably Christianity without discipleship," says Bonhoeffer. "It remains an abstract idea, a myth which has a place for the Fatherhood of God, but omits Christ as the living Son."

We must see the kingdom of heaven like the man who finds hidden treasure in a field. He reevaluates all of his priorities because nothing is as important as buying the field. We must become like that man, realizing everything else we have pales in comparison and so never look-ing back to the things that once were important (Matt. 13:44–50).

Where we have been loyal to many things, now we must be loyal to one thing: the person, Jesus Christ.

DAY 10

Radical Disobedience

So, because you are lukewarm—neither cold nor
hot—I am about to spit you out of my mouth.

—Revelation 3:16

"No other significance is possible,
since Jesus is the only significance."

—Dietrich Bonhoeffer

Jesus will not tolerate lukewarm, wishy-washy disciples. What we call radical obedience here on earth is actually the norm in the kingdom of heaven.

In other words, our lukewarm discipleship is actually radical disobedience. If radical discipleship is reflected by people who believe Jesus really means what he says, then what other choice is there?

A discipleship model for people who think Jesus may mean what he says but they're not sure?

A discipleship model for people who sort of agree with Jesus and sort of live according to his commands?

To become a disciple of Jesus means we move from rebellion against God to communion with God. There is no middle ground.

Being a disciple of Jesus doesn't mean simply agreeing with Jesus or even heading in the same general direction as Jesus. You can agree smoking is hazardous to your health, but your agreement means nothing until you stop smoking.

We're not called to a confession of faith or an intellectual agreement with biblical doctrine. Those may help us understand our commitment to Jesus, but the call of Jesus is to the Son of God himself.

DAY 11

Jesus Said 'Follow Me'

*As he walked along, he saw Levi son of Alphaeus sitting
at the tax collector's booth. "Follow me," Jesus told him.*

—MARK 2:14A

"Discipleship means adherence to Christ . . . an
abstract Christology, a doctrinal system, a general
religious knowledge on the subject of grace or on the
forgiveness of sins, render discipleship superfluous . . . ."

—DIETRICH BONHOEFFER

When Jesus calls Levi to follow, the command (*ako-
loutheô*) carries the sense of both one exclusive
path and becoming now and forever connected to that
path. Quite literally, it is a call to become part of the road.
In his brief expression, Jesus, in a sense, says, "I am the
WAY and I am calling you into a unique and unending
union with me, the one and only way."

But it is a command, and Bonhoeffer notes this forces
Levi into a choice. He can obey or disobey the command,
but he can't ignore it. In our negotiations with Jesus, we
fail to grasp that anything other than total obedience is

disobedience. There is no middle ground and our stalling, arguing, whining, and ignoring are all forms of disobedience. Our passive resistance is the same as rebellion against the commands of Jesus.

In our time, we speak of a radical obedience to Christ and we mean an extreme or fanatical faith where someone is committed to Jesus to the exclusion of anything or anyone else. We mean someone who sacrifices everything, who irrevocably alters his or her life in order to follow Jesus. The sacrifice is so high and so extreme there is no turning back.

We are amazed by their sacrifice and we assume they are exceptional Christians, but the truth is, their exceptional faith should be the norm, and what passes for normal in our congregations is little more than a general focus on Jesus that allows us to remain satisfied sitting at the threshold of Christian maturity without ever entering in to the abundant life Jesus died to provide.

Bonhoeffer says we've been lulled into believing that only certain people—monks, missionaries, and ministers—are called to be more saintly, while the rest of us can comfortably settle into a mediocre, part-time discipleship. Where are you in your pursuit of Jesus? Is it part-time, like a hobby? Or are you following in single-minded obedience? There is no condemnation in Christ; you can shift into full obedience at any moment.

DAY 12

Levi Got Up and Followed Him

"Follow me," Jesus told him, and Levi got up and followed him.
—MARK 2:14B

"If men imagine that they can follow Jesus
without taking [an actual step of obedience],
they are deluding themselves like fanatics."
—DIETRICH BONHOEFFER

What Jesus is trying to do, says Bonhoeffer, is to move us into a situation where faith is actually possible. In other words, a situation where we will fail unless Jesus comes through for us. If we can handle the situation on our own, then we will never develop faith—because we will not ever experience Jesus supplying our every need.

Jesus moves us to a place where the step of faith we take is irrevocable—if what Jesus says isn't true, then we are going down in flames; our step makes us totally dependent upon Jesus. Our decision to follow Jesus, then, becomes as irrevocable as the rich young man giving away all his wealth. His life will never be the same; he is totally dependent upon Jesus. He is in a place where he will see and experience, daily, that the promises of Jesus are true.

And, whether they are true or not, the rich young ruler cannot go back. Neither can we, if we walk by faith. "But we are not of those who shrink back and are destroyed, but of those who believe and are saved" (Heb. 10:39 TNIV), for "We live by faith, not by sight" (2 Cor. 5:7 TNIV).

Jesus doesn't call us to a step of faith in our mind, in which we simply agree intellectually that Jesus is Lord and maintain an abstract obedience to his commands. Jesus requires that we take tangible steps of faith that require us to trust him for the outcome.

But Bonhoeffer says this is where most of us stumble in our walk of faith. We agree, *in general*, to follow Jesus, but that doesn't mean we do in reality. We end up walking in a kind of *faithless Christianity*, where we are relatively good people trying to live good lives; but, that has nothing to do with following Jesus down the hard path through the narrow gate into the kingdom of heaven.

Jesus has called you to some specific step, but it scares you to death. Remember Jesus is at the other side of that step, calling you to obediently trust him and take the step. By taking the step, your trust (faith) in Jesus will grow. Like Peter, step out of the boat and plant your foot firmly on your faith in Jesus.

DAY 13

How Can We Know the Way?

Lord, we don't know where you are going,
so how can we know the way?

—JOHN 14:5

"Jesus goes on before to Jerusalem and to
the cross, and they are filled with fear and
amazement at the road he calls them to follow."

—DIETRICH BONHOEFFER

Do you realize that when you're not obedient to
Jesus, you're fighting against what is best for you?

Part of the strength God gives you to "do all things
through him" is the ability to choose to do his will, even
before you know the full implications of what that means.
He will begin to change your desire, developing within you
more and more of a "want" to do his will.

Am I willing to decide, in advance, that I will do what
God asks me to do, no matter what it is? Am I abandoned
to him and his will, believing he will strengthen me to do
all the things he asks? Or do I behave as if I believe I am
the final judge of what is best for my life: "God, show me

the whole plan, wait for me to understand, and then I'll decide whether or not to do what you ask"?

The Good News is that, even if you're not ready for immediate obedience, God will give you strength to be honest with him. He already knows about your hesitancy, so he won't be surprised by prayerful confessions, such as, "Father, I'm not sure I'm ready to do your will. I don't know if I want to do it or not."

Yet God is gracious and patient. Tell him, "I don't know that I'm willing to step out in faith without first knowing everything that's going to happen, but I'm willing to be made willing."

DAY 14

A Moment of No Return

"Lord, if it's you," Peter replied,
"tell me to come to you on the water." "Come," he said.

—MATTHEW 14:28–29A

"[The disciple's] old life seemed observable and
calculable, but in fact it was quite incalculable;
the new life seems unobservable and fortuitous,
but is in fact necessary and calculable."

—DIETRICH BONHOEFFER

The call of Jesus is a real and tangible command
that requires us to take a real and specific step in
response. Bonhoeffer says this first step of obedience
places us in a position where faith becomes possible.
Before the call, we are able to live life without faith. It may
even be a good and admirable life, but it is a faithless life.

To follow Jesus, we must have faith—a confident trust
in him. We cannot follow Jesus and try to remain in our
faithless life. We cannot get to where Jesus is taking us
unless we have this faith in him.

For example, Peter was in a storm-tossed boat when he saw Jesus walking on the water. Peter thought that if Jesus would just call him, he would be able to walk on the water, too. Jesus called, but Peter still had to decide to step out of the boat.

Thinking Jesus might give him the ability to walk on water was one thing, but it was quite another matter for Peter to actually trust Jesus would give him the ability. But the only way Peter could know was to step out of the boat. If his trust was well-placed, he would know for certain Jesus could do it. If his trust was ill-placed, then he would be floundering in the water.

Peter's step from the boat—the moment he put all his weight on the water—was a moment of no return. He would either sink or, not swim, but walk with Jesus. But note that Peter didn't just jump out of the boat; he waited for Jesus to call him out of the boat. And then his obedience put him in a place where his faith became real.

Is there a specific step Jesus has asked you to take? You will learn to trust him only as you take the step in obedience to his command.

DAY 15

Stepping into a New Life

"Come" he said. Then Peter got down out of the
boat, walked on the water and came toward Jesus.

—MATTHEW 14:29

"The disciple may think he is being dragged
out of his secure life into a life of absolute
insecurity, but in truth he is stepping into the
absolute security and safety of Jesus' fellowship."

—DIETRICH BONHOEFFER

When Peter stepped out of the storm-tossed boat
and onto the water, where was the safest place to
be? In the boat or in the arms of Jesus?

The answer, of course, is with Jesus, and for a brief
time, Peter saw that. Right then he got a glimpse of what
it is like to TRUST in Jesus and what it is like to operate
within the realm of costly grace as a citizen of the kingdom of heaven.

And we get a glimpse of that, too. We see that following Jesus requires us to step into apparent insecurity in
order to find true security. In the alleged insecurity of

discipleship, we experience the gift of Christ and are enveloped in the grace of God.

It's a paradox of faith: Our first step of faith places us in a position where faith becomes possible. By our obedience, we learn to be faithful. If we refuse to follow, we never learn how to believe. We stay stuck in the shallow end of faith, trusting in ourselves, living by sight and not by faith.

Bonhoeffer notes the step we take is itself inconsequential. We are saved by faith, not any action, even our step of faith. Jesus commands; we obey. You do not become a child of God through obedience, but by faith (Rom. 1:17).

Discipleship is Jesus constantly pushing us into new situations where it is possible for us to trust him even more. He pushes us into impossible situations where we must stake everything solely on his Word. Ask Jesus to push you to the place where you will know with certainty that he is good for his Word, that he is the Word of God.

DAY 16

Your Freedom Will Cost Me

*Going a little farther, he fell with his face to the ground
and prayed, "My Father, if it is possible, may this cup
be taken from me. Yet not as I will, but as you will."*

—MATTHEW 26:39

"Anybody living in the strength of Christ's
baptism lives in the strength of Christ's death."

—DIETRICH BONHOEFFER

If you asked most evangelical Christians to define
grace, they'd probably tell you it's the unmerited favor
of God. Not a bad answer, but one that's just academic
enough to keep you from staring straight into the face
of grace.

Grace is powerful, audacious, and dangerous, and if it
ever got free reign in our churches, it would begin a transformation so rapid and radical that it might cause skeptics
to beat a path to our door.

What is grace? Consider this illustration from *Les
Miserables*, Victor Hugo's timeless tale about a peasant
who is sentenced to hard labor for stealing a loaf of bread.

Released from jail, Jean Valjean is offered brief sanctuary in the home of a priest.

Despite being treated with dignity for the first time in years, Valjean, steals the bishop's valuable silverware and runs away. The next day, Valjean is brought back to the priest's home by the police, who tell the priest that Valjean has claimed the silver as a gift. The police obviously expect the priest to deny the claim.

The priest immediately addresses Valjean, saying, "Ah, there you are! I am glad to see you. But I gave you the candlesticks also, which are silver like the rest, and would bring two hundred francs. Why did you not take them along with your plates?" When he hands the candlesticks to Valjean privately, he tells him, "Jean Valjean, my brother, you belong no longer to evil, but to good. It is your soul that I am buying for you."

It's a Christ-like moment—and one that shows the tremendous cost of grace, both for the giver and the receiver.

This illustration echoes the story of the woman caught in adultery. When no one is willing to throw the first stone, Jesus says he will not condemn her either. "Go and sin no more," he says. Jesus knows what you've done; he still loves you. Hear him say, "I do not condemn you, but don't forget what your freedom has cost me. Now go and sin no more."

DAY 17

Did God Really Say That?

Now a man came up to Jesus and asked, "Teacher,
what good thing must I do to get eternal life?"

—MATTHEW 19:16

"The revealed commandment of God is
incomplete, he says, as he makes the last
attempt to preserve his independence and
decide for himself what is good and evil."

—DIETRICH BONHOEFFER

When the rich young man came to Jesus, the Lord
would not allow him to perpetuate the myth that
we can get to the God-life on our own terms. He won't
allow us to live in that myth either. He won't allow us to be
double-minded in discipleship, where we agree to follow
after Jesus but then get sidetracked—chasing hypotheti-
cal moral or intellectual dilemmas down trails that get
us nowhere nearer righteous living, let alone into the
kingdom of heaven.

Bonhoeffer suggests that our many "what ifs" about
discipleship keep us from the "necessity of obedience."

We get so wound up trying to understand each step along the way —or, like the rich young man, trying to figure out that one thing we must do—that we become enslaved by doubt. Yet our freedom is found in simple, single-minded obedience to Jesus.

We must do what we know we're supposed to do, and as we take each step of obedience, Jesus will reveal the next thing for us to do. Otherwise, we end up picking and choosing which commandments to obey, and our lingering debates lull us into thinking we are in a negotiation with Jesus when, in fact, we are simply disobeying him.

Bonhoeffer writes that the rich young man is actually attempting to "preserve his independence and decide for himself what is good and evil." And that echoes back to the Garden and the hiss of the snake: "Did God really say that?" Surely there must be more to this than what God says?

Ask Jesus to question you in the places where you remain independent of him. Where are you still trying to decide for yourself what is good and what is evil?

DAY 18

Loyalty to Cheap Grace

*Jesus answered, "If you want to be perfect, go, sell
your possessions and give to the poor, and you will
have treasure in heaven. Then come, follow me."*

—MATTHEW 19:21

"Here is the sum of the commandments—
to live in fellowship with Christ."

—DIETRICH BONHOEFFER

For the rich young man, the thing that held his loyalty more than anything else was his wealth. For us, it may be prestige or reputation, promotion or influence, friends or family. It may be an insistence that we must earn our way into God's good graces or it may be a deeply rooted delusion that following Jesus simply means we become nice people.

It may be a loyalty to cheap grace, where we think forgiveness of our sins is de facto permission to keep on living the way we always have. After all, Jesus forgives us.

No matter what it is, if we give it greater loyalty than we give Jesus, we are engaged in idolatry.

We are reluctant to give up these things that grip our attention because we think they provide us with a degree of security. In truth, what appears to be security is, in fact, insecurity—and what appears to be insecurity is, in truth, eternal security.

When Jesus called Peter to step out of the boat and walk to him across the water, it was a call to voluntarily give up the security of the boat for the insecurity of walking on rough water (Matt. 14:22–31). With single-minded obedience, Peter takes the first step, and in that moment, he believes. Obedience doesn't merely reflect belief; in truth, obedience leads to belief.

You cannot develop faith if you are disobedient to Jesus. You may give intellectual assent to what God can do but unless you take the first step, you do not have faith.

There is no other path than obedience to developing faith. Only by leaving the "security" of the boat does Peter discover that the greater security is in Jesus. Truth is, the only security is in Jesus.

What will change in your life now that you know the only true security is in Jesus?

DAY 19

Grace Is an Orchestra

For to me, to live is Christ and to die is gain.

—PHILIPPIANS 1:21

"Indeed it is wrong to speak of the Christian
life: we should speak rather of Christ living
in us . . . Christ, incarnate, crucified and
glorified, has entered my life and taken charge."

—DIETRICH BONHOEFFER

Grace is an orchestra you are invited to join. Your membership is free. It is a gift from the maestro who sees a talent in you no one else sees. But joining the orchestra will cost you everything because you have to leave other things behind as you focus on following the maestro and becoming the musician God made you to be.

The maestro will demand you give up anything that distracts, anything that hinders your progress, any habit or attitude that simply isn't fitting for the grand performance to come. The maestro will not compromise his standards of excellence; yet every day he will be by your side, encouraging you in your development as a musician.

When some join the symphony, they refuse to give up their presumptions of what it is like to play in the orchestra. Instead of following the maestro, they follow their own formulas for how the music should be played. This is legalism, and it is as much disobedience to the commands of Jesus as the rebellion we so easily cite as disobedience.

Others join the orchestra and assume they don't have to work hard at becoming better musicians. They remain sloppy in their technique and they bring their bad habits into the symphony. They have no regard for the gift the maestro gave them when he invited them to join the orchestra. Some of them assume they were invited to join because of their talents and abilities, not realizing they are only there from the word of the maestro.

This is cheap grace, and it assumes we need not put serious effort into following Jesus with an abandonment that includes throwing off "everything that hinders" including "the sin that so easily entangles" as we "run with perseverance the race marked out for us" (Heb. 12:1 tniv).

What gets in the way of your following Jesus with passionate, desperate determination?

DAY 20

When Speculation Replaces Faith

That was the last thing the young man expected to hear.
And so, crestfallen, he walked away. He was holding
on tight to a lot of things, and he couldn't bear to let go.

—MATTHEW 19:22 (MSG)

"It is a retreat from the reality of God to the
speculations of men, from faith to doubt."

—DIETRICH BONHOEFFER

Jesus demands we drop the distractions and become single-minded in our obedience to his commands. In the case of the rich young man, this requirement pulls him away from the romantic fantasy that Christ's commands are what Bonhoeffer calls a mere "opportunity for moral adventure, a thrilling way of life, but one which might easily be abandoned for another if occasion arose."

The young man is pulled into the reality of costly grace, where our only hope to enter the kingdom of heaven lies in Jesus Christ, our Lord. Jesus won't allow him to see eternal life as a distant dream; he insists he follow him into that life now, for "the kingdom of heaven is near" (Matt. 4:17).

Discipleship, Bonhoeffer says, is not the completion of an old life, doing that one final thing you have to do to enter the kingdom, like the capstone of a long and distinguished career that ushers you into retirement. Discipleship is about irrevocably leaving your present life behind and entering a new life, where Jesus is the center of significance.

It is a life in which Jesus is the only significance.

Bonhoeffer says, "Here is the sum of the commandments—to live in fellowship with Christ." Jesus must bring us to the place where we abandon anything that holds us to the old life, anything other than Jesus to which we are attached.

The attachments may be different for different people. For the rich young man, the attachment was to his wealth. What are the attachments you have that keep you part-time in your pursuit of Christ?

DAY 21

Counting the Cost

As they were walking along the road, a man said to
him, "I will follow you wherever you go." Jesus replied,
"Foxes have holes and birds of the air have nests,
but the Son of Man has no place to lay his head."

—LUKE 9:57–58

"The first disciple offers to follow Jesus without
waiting to be called. Jesus damps his ardour by
warning him that he does not know what he is doing."

—DIETRICH BONHOEFFER

Jesus demands obedience from his disciples, but he also
expects us to count the cost of our commitment (Luke
14:28–30). Bonhoeffer says disciples with a romantic
view of following Christ volunteer to go anywhere at any
time, but their commitment fails when things become
inconvenient—or when they collide with the full cost
of discipleship.

Discipleship means we give up any thought that there
will be bits and pieces of our lives that can remain unaf-
fected by our relationship with Jesus. We no longer have

the choice to serve where we want in the way we want and still be home in bed by 10:00. We no longer have the luxury of deciding our future based upon a 401K and a dental plan.

Can you imagine the Apostle Paul deciding where to go next based on the cost of living in a particular town? Why should we be any different? We serve the same Lord; we're infused with the same Holy Spirit. Are the standards of discipleship different now than they were in the first century A.D.? Are we called to a lesser discipleship? Do we serve a lesser Lord?

When we have a romantic view of discipleship, we may imagine ourselves giving up everything for Jesus as the world admires our faith and people express their heartfelt gratitude for our sacrificial service.

But the cost of discipleship will likely be the scorn of a world that sees you throwing away your future to help people who can give you nothing in return. Discipleship may mean sacrificing for others who will have no appreciation for what you have done—much like Jesus, who was ridiculed as he died on a cross.

The grace to go wherever Jesus tells us to go comes only through the call of Christ and the power of God infused into our being. Grace only comes to us as we obey Jesus, regardless of the circumstances or consequences.

How much of your service to Jesus is based upon what is convenient for you and how much of it is based upon you doing what Jesus tells you to do?

DAY 22

Focus on Jesus, Not the Law

He said to another man, "Follow me." But the man
replied, "Lord, first let me go and bury my father."
Jesus said to him, "Let the dead bury their own
dead, but you go and proclaim the kingdom of God."

—LUKE 9:59–60

"Christ calls, the disciple follows: that
is grace and commandment in one."

—DIETRICH BONHOEFFER

We're called to focus on Jesus, not the law. Yet, like this disciple, we often say to Jesus, the law-giver, "Let me do what I'm supposed to and then come follow you."

Jesus replies, in a sense, "Don't use the law as an excuse to not follow me. Don't put the law above me."

We follow the law by following Jesus. We cannot earn our own righteousness, and so we connect to Jesus and his righteousness. Jesus did follow the law perfectly, and our connection to him wraps us in his cloak of righteousness.

"For he has clothed me with garments of salvation and arrayed me in a robe of righteousness. . ." (Isa. 61:10).

This means we must give Jesus priority over everything and everyone in our lives.

- When we are faced with a choice between what *appears* to us to be good and Jesus, we must follow Jesus obediently, trusting that he is the "good" we should follow.
- When we are faced with a choice between what *appears* to us to be right ("this relationship just feels right to me") and Jesus, we must choose Jesus trusting that he is the "right" we should follow.
- When we face a choice between loyalty to someone or something and Jesus, we must choose Jesus. "Anyone who comes to me but refuses to let go of father, mother, spouse, children, brothers, sisters—yes, even one's own self!—can't be my disciple" (Luke 14:26 MSG).

Jesus wants to empty us of our self-interest so he can fill us with himself. Only then can we love others in the way Jesus loves us.

DAY 23

Looking Back Is Double-mindedness

Still another said, "I will follow you, Lord; but first let me go back and say good-bye to my family." Jesus replied, "No one who puts his hand to the plow and looks back is fit for service in the kingdom of God."

—LUKE 9:61–62

"By making his offer on his own terms, [this disciple] alters the whole position, for discipleship can tolerate no conditions which might come between Jesus and our obedience to him."

—DIETRICH BONHOEFFER

When we follow Jesus, we cannot stipulate our own terms. Discipleship is not, Bonhoeffer notes, like a career we map out for ourselves: "I'll do this for Jesus after I get the kids through school and build my retirement fund." We cannot arrange things to suit ourselves; otherwise, Bonhoeffer says, we end up serving Jesus "in accordance with the standards of a rational ethic."

This still leaves us in control, deciding our service on what makes sense. We may accomplish good things but that doesn't make us disciples of Jesus. He said, "No one who puts a hand to the plow and looks back is fit for service in the kingdom of God" (Luke 9:62 TNIV).

Looking back is double-mindedness. It makes us unstable and uncertain and that's the exact opposite of the focused following Jesus expects of us. It means there are moments in our relationship with Jesus when we say, "I'll get back to you, Jesus, just as soon as I finish with my priorities."

It is the creature putting the Creator on hold.

DAY 24

Teaching and Fulfilling the Law

*Anyone who breaks one of the least of these commandments
and teaches others to do the same will be called least in the
kingdom of heaven, but whoever practices and teaches these
commands will be called great in the kingdom of heaven.*

—MATTHEW 5:19

"Only the doer of the law can
remain in communion with Jesus."

—DIETRICH BONHEOFFER

Bonhoeffer says the Pharisees remind us "that it is
possible to teach the law without fulfilling it, to
teach it in such a way that it cannot be fulfilled."

Jesus will have none of that. He expects us to obey the
law just as he did. Since Jesus fulfilled the law, if we follow
Jesus and become Christ-like, we will find ourselves obeying and teaching the law – even though we live within the
realm of costly grace. In the sense that we are in union
with Christ, we will find ourselves fulfilling the law, even
as we live under grace.

Bonhoeffer notes, "Only the doer of the law can remain in communion with Jesus."

We must move from merely being teachers of the word to being doers of the word. We no longer just study the word; we become it. As we submit ourselves to the Word that lives within us, we are transformed by grace and conformed to his image.

By virtue of our union with Christ in us, we are what we could never otherwise become. We become righteous because—and only because—the one in whom we abide is the very incarnation of holiness.

This is real righteousness—true holiness—because we are one with holy Christ and we obey our Lord when he commands. Then, as Romans 12:2 says, we no longer are conformed to this world, but transformed by the renewing of our minds, and able to "prove what the will of God is, that which is good and acceptable and perfect" (nas).

When we are in union with Christ and obey his commands, we do the will of God and fulfill the law of God. We transcend the teaching of the law and become doers of the law of Christ.

This is the way our righteousness exceeds the righteousness of the Pharisees. It is based exclusively on our communion with Jesus, the only one who fulfilled the law.

DAY 25

Don't Start Worrying

So do not worry, saying, "What shall we eat?" or
"What shall we drink?" or "What shall we wear?"

—MATTHEW 6:31

"If our hearts are set on [earthly possessions], our reward
is an anxiety whose burden is intolerable. Anxiety creates
its own treasures and they in turn beget further care."

—DIETRICH BONHOEFFER

The more we possess, the more we have to care for
our possessions, and that leads to our possessions
eventually possessing us. Jesus doesn't forbid us to have
possessions. His point is that we should not allow our possessions to get in the way of following him—and the more
we accumulate, the more likely we are to worry about how
we will pay for, take care of, keep, and protect the things
we own.

It leads to a cycle of always putting off our total abandonment to Jesus. We think, "When I get this much in the
bank, then I'll focus more on ministry. If I could just get

a bigger house, then I'd be able to host a small group in my home."

And that leads to scenarios in which we are unable to respond to Jesus because we're weighed down with worry and regret and too much stuff. We're unable to volunteer—that is, do the ministry Jesus calls us to do—because we have to work extra hours to pay for the things we have. We sense Jesus telling us to step out in faith to pursue a different career, one that matches the way he has shaped us for ministry – but then we think, "I can't quit my job, Jesus, I have a mortgage to pay."

Jesus enters into our thinking, where we load ourselves down with obligations he never intended for us to carry and create worry that distracts us from following him faithfully. Suddenly, we're serving things instead of serving Jesus. We begin to believe, "It is all up to me to pay for these things and to provide for my needs and my family's needs." And that is fallen thinking locked into the economy of this world. Jesus says in God's economy, in the kingdom of heaven, our Father is the provider and he knows our needs better than we do ourselves.

Look around, look at how he provides. Now believe he will provide for you.

DAY 26

Everything Comes from God

What I'm trying to do here is to get you to relax, to not be so
preoccupied with getting, so you can respond to God's giving.
People who don't know God and the way he works fuss over
these things, but you know both God and how he works.

—MATTHEW 6:31–32 (MSG)

"According to [Jesus], bread is not to be valued
as the reward for work; he speaks instead of the
carefree simplicity of the man who walks with him
and accepts everything as it comes from God."

—DIETRICH BONHEOFFER

Bonhoeffer notes that the birds and the lilies "glorify
their Creator, not by their industry, toil or care, but
by a daily unquestioning acceptance of his gifts." A characteristic of fallen thinking is the assumption that there
is a "cause and effect between work and sustenance, but
Jesus explodes that illusion."

Jesus topples the mythology that what you do is a mea-
sure of what you are worth, which is just another variation
on the mythology of earning your way into God's good

graces. This is one way we cheapen grace because we say the work of Jesus provides for our salvation, but it doesn't have anything to do with our survival or sustenance here on earth.

Jesus says anxiety is characteristic of those who do not believe in God. "They do not know that the Father knows that we have need of all these things, and so they try to do for themselves what they do not expect from God," says Bonhoeffer.

How many of us are practicing pagans, claiming faith in Jesus but behaving like atheists? We're paralyzed with worry and fear, unwilling to trust Jesus. Do you believe that if you follow Jesus, you will lack nothing? Is the issue with you or with God?

How would our congregations change if we made it absolutely understandable that worry is a sin? When we worry, we mock the words of Christ. "Surely," we think, "Jesus didn't know what he was talking about when he told us not to worry. Of course, we have to worry!"

How would your life change if you asked God to teach you not to worry? If you said, "God, keep me focused on this until I finally trust you"?

DAY 27

Getting Past Our Human Nature

But when Jesus turned and looked at his disciples, he
rebuked Peter. "Get behind me, Satan!" he said. "You do
not have in mind the things of God, but the things of men

—MARK 8:33

"Jesus says that every Christian has his own cross waiting
for him, a cross destined and appointed by God."

—DIETRICH BONHOEFFER

When Jesus calls you, he expects you to begin thinking like him. This isn't as impossible as it sounds because the Apostle Paul says you have been given the mind of Christ: "'Who has known the mind of the Lord so as to instruct him?' But we have the mind of Christ" (1 Cor. 2:16 TNIV).

The issue is in accessing the mind of Christ as you mediate upon God's Word and listen to the Holy Spirit, who is your guide into all truth (John 16:13). If you imagine discipleship as a physical journey, then you can easily see that the more time you spend with Jesus, the more you will begin to understand his way of thinking.

As you walk with him day in and day out, you will become intimate with his likes and dislikes; you will see what he sees and hear what he hears. You will know what he cares about and you will know what he considers insignificant, petty, or distracting. You will witness how he responds to problems, expectations, and laughter, and you will learn what he thinks about your future.

All of this will teach you to think from God's perspective, to engage the mind of Christ available to you through the Holy Sprit.

The Apostle Peter shows how this transformation takes place. As he follows Jesus, he begins to submit his mind to the Father and that changes his perspective. He begins to see things as they appear inside the kingdom of heaven.

In other words, Peter begins to clearly see reality and he is able to see the truth that Jesus is the Messiah. Jesus says, "For this was not revealed to you by man, but by my Father in heaven" (Matt. 16:17).

DAY 28

Bearing the Sins of Others

We always carry around in our body the death of Jesus, so that the life of Jesus may also be revealed in our body. For we who are alive are always being given over to death for Jesus' sake, so that his life may be revealed in our mortal body. So then, death is at work in us, but life is at work in you.

—2 CORINTHIANS 4:10–12

"Just as Christ is Christ only in virtue of his suffering and rejection, so the disciple is a disciple only in so far as he shares his Lord's suffering and rejection and crucifixion."

—DIETRICH BONHOEFFER

The cost of discipleship, then, is this: The way we become like Jesus is through suffering and rejection. Bonhoeffer says, "For God is a God who bears. The Son of God bore our flesh, he bore the cross, he bore our sins, thus making atonement for us. In the same way his followers are also called upon to bear, and that is precisely what it means to be a Christian."

Jesus isn't speaking about the watered-down sort of cross-bearing we so readily accept today, where we speak of the obnoxious neighbor, the dwindling asset, or the occasional migraine as daily crosses we must bear. Bonhoeffer notes that comparing the standard "trials and tribulations" of life with the bloody death of Jesus reduces his cross to an "every day calamity" and suggests the gospel is nothing more than a means to feeling good about our circumstances.

Certainly, we're meant to bear the obnoxious shortcomings of others; the things that annoy us about them. But when Jesus says we must bear our cross daily, he means we must bear the sins of others just as he bore our sins. This is how God brings out the life of Christ planted in us by the Holy Spirit and it enables us to take the deep regrets and loss in our lives, those past and present, and view them as God's way of acquainting us with the grief, heartache, and sorrow Jesus experienced on his way to the cross.

In this way, Paul says, the death of Christ is at work in us so that the life of Christ can be at work in others.

DAY 29

Every Command of Jesus
Is a Call to Die

*Then he called the crowd to him along with his disciples
and said: "If anyone would come after me, he must
deny himself and take up his cross and follow me."*

—MARK 8:34

"Every command of Jesus is a call to die—
we die to our own 'affections and lusts.'"

—DIETRICH BONHOEFFER

Jesus brings the disciples to a choice. He will not force
them to suffer. They can follow him or choose not to
follow him, but that means they reject him.

And this is why Jesus so often addresses the weary and
brokenhearted. Such people are often ready to suffer for
a worthwhile cause. They alone understand God will give
them "treasures of darkness and riches from secret places,
so that you may know that I, the Lord, the God of Israel
call you by your name" (Isa. 45:3 HCSB).

Bonhoeffer notes our death—the way we join with the
death of Jesus; the way we carry his death within us (2

Cor. 4:10)—may be leaving home or the place we work, like the first disciples did to follow Jesus. Or it may be leaving the comfort and predictability of tradition, such as when the monk Martin Luther left the monastery.

"But it is the same death every time—death in Jesus Christ, the death of the old man at his call," says Bonhoeffer. Every day we are given a choice to obey or not obey Jesus as we fight with sin and the devil.

DAY 30

Called to an Extraordinary Life

We can understand someone dying for a person worth dying for, and we can understand how someone good and noble could inspire us to selfless sacrifice. But God put his love on the line for us by offering his Son in sacrificial death while we were of no use whatever to him.

—ROMANS 5:7–8 (MSG)

"To endure the cross is not a tragedy; it is the suffering which is the fruit of an exclusive allegiance to Jesus Christ. When it comes, it is not an accident, but a necessity."

—DIETRICH BONHOEFFER

If suffering and rejection lead to intimacy with the Father, could it be the inability of so many of us to go deeper with God is our fear of suffering and rejection? Is it possible our avoidance of these things keeps us in the shallow waters of discipleship?

As we learn to think like Jesus, Bonhoeffer says our perspective on suffering and rejection will change from fearful avoidance to redemptive endurance. We will come to understand that enduring the cross is not a tragedy;

rather, it is the fruit of "an exclusive allegiance to Jesus Christ."

In that light, any rejection of suffering by a disciple means the rejection of Jesus. When we avoid suffering and rejection, for instance, by chasing after little gods of compromise, we are denying Christ no less audibly than when Peter, standing next to the servants of Caiaphas by the courtyard fire, insisted he was not a disciple of Jesus.

Jesus always brings us to a choice as he watches the doomsday clock count down. The road is narrow and the gate is narrow into the kingdom of heaven.

- Are you willing to suffer?
- Are you prepared to be rejected?

The student is not greater than the master and the master is calling you to follow him into the kingdom, regardless of the suffering and rejection this may bring.

DAY 31

The Cross Gives Us
the Power to Forgive

*So if you forgive him, I forgive him. Don't think I'm carrying
around a list of personal grudges. The fact is that I'm joining
in with your forgiveness, as Christ is with us, guiding us.*

—2 CORINTHIANS 2:10 (MSG)

"My brother's burden which I must bear is not
only his outward lot, his natural characteristics
and gifts, but quite literally his sin."

—DIETRICH BONHOEFFER

We're called to bear the sins of others—the things
they do that cost us—just as Jesus bore our sins
even when there was no guarantee we'd ever notice, appre-
ciate, or even care about his sacrifice. In truth, there was
no guarantee we'd even stop incurring more cost for him
to bear (Rom. 5:8).

Bonhoeffer says the only way we can "bear that sin is by
forgiving it in the power of the cross of Christ in which
[we] now share." He says forgiving others is the Christ-like
suffering we are called to bear, and this requires another

shift in our thinking because it destroys any fantasy that forgiveness is all about "being nice" and "can't we all just get along."

Forgiveness is a bloody work that costs, not only the life of Jesus, but your life as well: "For whoever wants to save their life will lose it, but whoever loses their life for me will save it" (Mat 16:25). Grace is free, but it isn't cheap. If every time we sinned, we could hear the clank of hammer to nail through wrist, the devil would have a hard time moving his inventory of sin.

It is bearing the sins of others, even when it means suffering and rejection, that creates the distinction between "an ordinary human life and a life committed to Christ," says Bonhoeffer.

To echo the Apostle Paul, "We can understand someone dying for a person worth dying for, and we can understand how someone good and noble could inspire us to selfless sacrifice" (Rom. 5:7 MSG), but to forgive others, even when it means suffering and rejection, who could do that but someone compelled by the power of God?

DAY 32

Take This Suffering Away

For the joy set before him he endured the cross.

—HEBREWS 12:2

"The cross is not the terrible end to an otherwise
godfearing and happy life, but it meets us at
the beginning of our communion with Christ."

—DIETRICH BONHOEFFER

Jesus prays for the cup of suffering to pass, and
Bonhoeffer observes it does pass, but only after Jesus
has gone through the suffering. His suffering is not per-
manent, but for the joy set before him, Jesus "endured the
cross, scorning its shame, and sat down at the right hand
of the throne of God" (Heb. 12:2).

Jesus trusted in God's promise, he trusted his suffering
would end, and he trusted his suffering not only served a
purpose, but would also lead to the end of suffering: "He
will wipe every tear from their eyes. There will be no more
death or mourning or crying or pain, for the old order of
things has passed away" (Rev. 21:4).

When we suffer, we can cling to the truth that God is not surprised. We do not suffer outside the sovereignty and power of God. We can rest in his promise that he has our best interests at heart, and when suffering and rejection come, we can TRUST that our suffering is not an accident but is a necessity that God uses to lovingly squeeze the things out of us that we might otherwise ignore or excuse—things like sin, disobedience, or apathy—the things that will get us flagged by security at the gates of the kingdom of heaven.

DAY 33

Submit to God, Not Goodness

Shouldn't we expect far greater glory under the new way,
now that the Holy Spirit is giving life? If the old way,
which brings condemnation, was glorious, how much more
glorious is the new way, which makes us right with God!

—2 CORINTHIANS 3:8–9 (NLT)

"Instead of calling us to follow Christ, [cheap
grace] has hardened us in our disobedience."

—DIETRICH BONHOEFFER

Jesus doesn't care if you are a good person.

When he calls you to follow him, he isn't asking you
to become a nice person and to do your best at helping
others. He didn't die so you could feel good about the
things you've screwed-up or so you could carry some sen-
timental hope of being reunited beyond the veil with the
people and pets you love but who have died.

His call is a command for you to abandon your life
and to follow him down an exclusive path and through
a narrow gate that leads to the kingdom of heaven.

Your entry into the kingdom is free, but you must leave everything behind in order to pass through the gate.

Understand this: Jesus doesn't demand that you give him all the things you leave behind, so leaving them behind isn't an entry fee you pay to enter the kingdom of heaven. His grace is free but you have to open your hands to receive it, and that requires you to let go of whatever else you are holding in your hands.

The first thing you have to let go of is the illusion that following Jesus is about becoming a nice person. Otherwise, you're just going to keep trying to make yourself nice by following a list of Sunday school rules that are self-righteous attempts to enter the kingdom of heaven on your own power, somewhere separate and away from the Jesus gate.

Or, you're going to keep mistaking the doctrine of grace for a doctrine of being nice, where following Jesus is all about "going along to get along" and an attitude of "nobody's perfect" will become your response to sin.

On the surface, both of these approaches look a bit like following Jesus, and that's why so many Christians are trapped in their shallowness.

Follow Jesus, and he will transform you from a good person into a godly one.

DAY 34

Sometime Obedience

Knowing the correct password—saying "Master, Master," for instance—isn't going to get you anywhere with me. What is required is serious obedience—doing what my Father wills.

—MATTHEW 7:21 (MSG)

"We can only achieve perfect liberty and enjoy fellowship with Jesus when his command, his call to absolute discipleship, is appreciated in its entirety."

—DIETRICH BONHOEFFER

Good afternoon; it's so good to see you again. How are the washer and dryer working out for you? What's that? Let me make sure I understand: You're saying they aren't working properly? No worries! Here at the Cheap Grace Appliance and Application Center, we pride ourselves on being able to give sometimes-support to our customers. And today, you're fortunate: it's one of the days we offer support!

Okay, tell me what's wrong. Ah, there's the problem— your expectations are too high! When you push the "start" button on any of our washers and dryers, they're only obedient to that command fifty percent of the time. The fact that your appliances follow your directions fifty-nine percent of the time is absolutely amazing. It simply isn't going to get any better than that.

It's like cheap grace. Nobody expects anybody to follow the commands of Jesus more than sixty percent of the time. Otherwise, we'd be fanatics, right? And, like our washing machines, if we all keep the expectations low, then none of us will feel too much pressure, know what I mean?

What? Your washer? Right, right—the owner's manual says the spin cycle will always follow the wash and rinse, but I'm afraid only thirty-seven percent of our washers pay attention to "the book." But, this should please you—a full fifty-eight of our washers admit that, when they don't respond to the command functions, they're doing wrong. You could say they're sinning instead of spinning. Ha, ha—oh, sorry, just a little service and support humor.

Well, I'm glad I could explain all of this to you. Thanks for coming by—say, is that a mustard stain on your shirt?

DAY 35

The Totality of Discipleship

*If anyone comes to me and does not hate his father
and mother, his wife and children, his brothers and
sisters—yes, even his own life—he cannot be my disciple.*

—LUKE 14:26

"By virtue of his incarnation [Jesus] has come
between man and his natural life. There can
be no turning back, for Christ bars the way."

—DIETRICH BONHOEFFER

The call of Jesus isolates us from family, friends,
nationality, and tradition—and that is exactly how
God intends it. Jesus calls you, not a group. He requires
that you stand alone before him in an intimate, face-to-
face relationship.

You are responsible for your decision to follow or not
follow him. You are responsible for your own obedience or
disobedience. Absolutely no one can stand between you
and Jesus and that is why he sounds so stern when he says
that we cannot be his disciples unless we love him more
than all others.

There is a totality in the cost of discipleship that demands an uncompromising loyalty. Jesus will not share your affection for him with anyone else, not even your family. If you are faced with a choice between loyalty to him and loyalty to your father or mother, sister or brother, you must choose Jesus or you cannot claim to be his disciple.

His expectation is so strict that, when faced with a choice between the interests of Jesus and your own self-interests, you must choose Jesus or you must admit you are no disciple to him at all.

Think about Peter warming his hands by the fire, just before the cock crows. Will he choose for Jesus or choose for himself? A disciple of Jesus is faced with the same decision every day.

Holy Jesus, meek and mild is about the serious business of salvation, and he has no time for split loyalties or uncertain commitments. Any relationship you have that jeopardizes your relationship with Jesus must be sacrificed.

His demand may seem unreasonable, yet Oswald Chambers says we should never try to interpret these words as separate from the Son of God who spoke them.

DAY 36

Tablets of the Heart

This "letter" is written not with pen and ink,
but with the Spirit of the living God. It is carved
not on tablets of stone, but on human hearts.

—2 CORINTHIANS 3:3 (NLT)

"Because between the disciples and the law
stands one who has perfectly fulfilled it,
one with whom they live in communion."

—DIETRICH BONHOEFFER

When God gave Moses the law, He said, "Take this down to the people. This is what I am like, and if they will keep this law, I will be their God and they will be my people." Moses went down and read the law to the Jewish people.

The late Christian educator Dan Stone said once they heard the law, they should have said, "We can't do that! That's what God is like. Those are *his* characteristics." But instead they said, "Okay, we can do it. We'll do it."

The Old Testament is a history of the fact that they couldn't do it.

We're no different. We get "saved," grab the Bible and say, "We'll do it!" And we haven't done it, either.

How did they serve God in the Old Testament? By keeping the law and offering sacrifices and periodically asking for their sins to be forgiven.

How do we try to serve God? By keeping the law, and offering sacrifices—trying to make up for the things we've done wrong—and then asking for forgiveness because we've failed.

But that's not the way it's supposed to work. The Old Testament prophets knew that. They knew God didn't want the blood of bulls and goats, but a contrite heart. Instead, God writes the rules "not on tablets of stone, but on human hearts" (2 Cor. 3:3 NLT).

Jesus wants the way you live your life as a Christian to become as spontaneous as it was when you were "lost." In other words, he wants you to live from the life he places in you and not from a list of rules that go no deeper than changing your appearance and behavior.

DAY 37

Think Small and Travel Light

[L]et us throw off everything that hinders and
the sin that so easily entangles, and let us run
with perseverance the race marked out for us.

—HEBREWS 12:1B

"If, for instance, we give away all our possessions, that
act is not in itself the obedience he demands . . . we
might then be choosing a way of life for ourselves."

—DIETRICH BONHOEFFER

When Jesus tells us to break with our old existence, his command is not arbitrary or random. You could say it is meant to make us small enough to fit through the narrow gate that leads to the kingdom of heaven. Imagine trying to go down a narrow path and then through a narrow gate wearing a backpack overstuffed with heavy regrets from your past and superficial distractions from the present.

You'd end up exhausted and frustrated as your backpack and the things spilling out of it kept getting snagged on the narrow sides of the path. You'd begin to see many of the things you carried were a hindrance rather than a help, and one-by-one, you'd start tossing them aside.

How would you feel when you got to the end of the path and found out the only way you could fit through the gate was to leave behind everything you still had with you, even your backpack? So you reluctantly throw it off and head through the gate, only to discover that everything you'd been carrying, everything you'd been so reluctant to leave behind, would have been useless in your new life in the kingdom of heaven.

Inside the kingdom of heaven, you realize you made your journey more difficult than it had to be simply because you kept trying to hold on to things that were impossible to keep.

This is why Jim Elliot, who was killed while attempting to evangelize the Waodani people in Ecuador, wrote, "He is no fool who gives up what he cannot keep to gain what he cannot lose."

DAY 38

Your Relationships Must Change

Let us, therefore, make every effort to enter that rest . . . .
—HEBREWS 4:11A

"Beside Jesus nothing has any
significance. He alone matters."
—DIETRICH BONHOEFFER

We believe Jesus is the path, the way to the Father. We believe his death and resurrection created the bridge for us to cross into the kingdom of heaven.

But Jesus also clears the path by insisting we "throw off everything that hinders and the sin that so easily entangles" (Heb. 12:1).

He appears ruthless as he demands we give preference to him over anyone else, including the greatest love of your life, your best friend, your romantic dreams, even your own mother.

But we misunderstand Jesus if we think his ruthlessness emerges from mean-spiritedness or self-interest. Jesus has the endgame in mind, and he wants us with him in heaven, so he insists we re-center around his image.

Truth is never defined by appearances. Note that in the oft-quoted Jeremiah 29:11, God tells us that we may think he's leading us toward disaster, but his plans will actually "prosper [us] and not [harm us] . . . give [us] hope and a future" (Jer. 29:11).

We will change as we trust in Jesus to look out for us and, as we walk in this trust, we will see Jesus consistently come through for us one time after another and another and another. Through this, we see he not only keeps his promises, but he is powerful enough to keep his promises, and that helps us trust him more as the risks we must take in faith increase. We come to the point where we know he will be there on the other side of our step of faith.

The key to change is not working through a list of behaviors, although that certainly can help. We are changed by getting to know Jesus. He is the power to change us (Rom. 4:21; Rom. 1:16–17; 1 Cor. 1:17–19). Our job is to rest in his costly grace (Heb. 4:8–11).

DAY 39

We Are 'One with Christ'

*Through him all things were made; without
him nothing was made that has been made. In
him was life, and that life was the light of men.*

—John 1:3–4

"Since the whole world was created through him and
unto him . . . he is the sole Mediator in the world."

—Dietrich Bonhoeffer

Jesus is the mediator between you and God. Your intimacy with him allows you to be intimate with God, but you cannot disconnect that intimacy when you interact with others. You are a unit of "one with Christ" and so, as Bonhoeffer explains, Jesus is not only the mediator between you and God, he also becomes the mediator between you and other people, and between you and reality.

The cost of discipleship is that from now on, the only way you can relate to anyone is as "one with Christ." This doesn't mean merely making others aware you are connected to Christ; it means, to echo C. S. Lewis in *Mere*

Christianity, recognizing the reality that each person you relate to is an eternal being who will spend eternity in one of two places: the kingdom of heaven or the wards of hell.

Your ability to love others, to respond to them as eternal beings, comes from your connection with Jesus (1 John 4:11–12). When you try to relate to them in any other way, you are trying to relate as if you are no longer connected to Jesus. And when you do that, you're no longer leaning on Jesus as mediator or following him as a disciple.

That's the danger in cheap grace. We assume that since we are forgiven, we can now go back and relate to others as if we are not connected to Jesus. But we can't do that anymore than someone who's just gotten married can go back to former lovers and try to maintain a relationship with them that does not recognize the marriage. We are in union with Jesus just as a married man and woman are in union with each other.

When we try to separate Jesus from our relationships, we are denying reality and undermining the authenticity of those relationships. Have you tried to put Jesus in a box, compartmentalizing him away from certain relations?

What will you do about that now?

DAY 40

An Extraordinary Life

Go in through the narrow gate, because the gate to hell
is wide and the road that leads to it is easy, and there
are many who travel it. But the gate to life is narrow and
the way that leads to it is hard, and there are few people
who find it. Enter through the narrow gate. For wide is
the gate and broad is the road that leads to destruction,
and many enter through it. But small is the gate and
narrow the road that leads to life, and only a few find it.

—MATTHEW 7:13–14

"To be called to a life of extraordinary quality, to live up to
it, and yet to be unconscious of it is indeed a narrow way."

—DIETRICH BONHOEFFER

Jesus says his kingdom comes to give us an extraordinary life. God wants to bless us, not curse us, but we
must come to him on his terms, not ours.

It is a life we will live in intimate connection with the
God of the universe. "Father, just as you are in me and I
am in you," Jesus says, "[m]ay they also be in us so that
the world may believe that you have sent me. I have given

them the glory that you gave me, that they may be one as we are one—I in them and you in me—so that they may be brought to complete unity. Then the world will know that you sent me and have loved them even as you have loved me" (John 17:21–23 TNIV).

Jesus wipes away any thoughts that we can live this life independent of God. We are called to do things that are impossible for mere humans, and so we should expect that we will be constantly pushed into positions that require faith. If we are living a life that does not require faith, then we are not living the life of a disciple. If we are living a life that does not require faith, then we are living faithlessly.

He calls us to a life of total dependency on him, but it is not a dependency of weakness. If we say a man is dependent upon air, we don't consider his dependency a weakness. We understand that the air sustains his life.

And this isn't just an Everyman sitting on the mountain. Jesus isn't just a teacher. Here is the God of the universe, incarnated as the Son of God, looking across the crowd with the eyes of compassion. The Creator looking upon his creations, whom he loves.

He doesn't see their dependence as weakness. He sees it as strength; he sees it as intimacy; he sees it as natural, exactly how he created them to be.

And if we had his eyes, we would see it that way too, and so he sets to work to give us the ability to see through his eyes.

DAY 41

Becoming Desperate for God

*Blessed are the poor in spirit, for
theirs is the kingdom of heaven.*

—MATTHEW 5:3

"Now [the disciples] are poor—so
inexperienced, so stupid, that they have
no other hope but him who called them."

—DIETRICH BONHOEFFER

Jesus says, "God blesses those who are poor and realize their need for him, for the Kingdom of Heaven is theirs" (Matt. 5:3 NLT). He means we must come to the end of ourselves. We have to leave behind any self-sufficiency or self-righteousness and come to the place where we realize our only hope is in Jesus Christ, our Lord.

We must be desperate for God: "You're blessed when you're at the end of your rope. With less of you there is more of God and his rule" (Matt. 5:3 MSG).

Bonhoeffer notes the original disciples did not have religious wealth, in the sense that they did not have Pharisaical prestige or position.

And, as they followed Jesus, they were inexperienced in this new way. All they could do was follow Jesus for each next step; they couldn't rely on well-worn traditions that are so easily leaned upon in place of a relationship with Jesus.

They had nowhere else to turn but to Jesus—and it should be that way for us, as well.

If you really believed there was no where else to turn but Jesus, how would your life change?

DAY 42

Keeping an Eye on the Endgame

Blessed are those who mourn, for they will be comforted.
—MATTHEW 5:4

"[Jesus] means refusing to be in tune with the
world or to accommodate oneself to its standards."
—DIETRICH BONHOEFFER

Jesus says his disciples will see the world as it is.

They will see the ship is beginning to sink. "The world dreams of progress, of power and of the future, but the disciples meditate on the end, the last judgment, and the coming of the kingdom," says Bonhoeffer

The disciples of Jesus will have their eyes on the last judgment and that will not only change the way they live, it will cause them to mourn the darkness and decay of the world, to bear a sorrow for those who are dancing toward death instead of redemption and to bear the cost that comes their way because they follow Jesus.

"Sorrow cannot tire them or wear them down," Bonhoeffer says. "It cannot embitter them or cause them to break down under the strain; far from it, for they bear their sorrow in the strength of him who bears them up, who bore the whole suffering of the world upon the cross."

They will begin to see what Jesus sees—a world in need of a savior; people in desperate need of a loving Shepherd—and that will motivate them to break from the world in order to work with Jesus on his mission to save the world.

Jesus says, "You're blessed when you feel you've lost what is most dear to you. Only then can you be embraced by the One most dear to you" (Matt. 5:4 MSG).

DAY 43

We Cease to Be Strangers

Blessed are the meek, for they will inherit the earth.

—Matthew 5:5

"Those who now possess it by violence and injustice shall lose it, and those who here have utterly renounced it, who were meek to the point of the cross, shall rule the new earth."

—Dietrich Bonhoeffer

Jesus says his disciples will be blessed if they are humble. We are humble when we understand who we are and who we belong to.

Bonhoeffer says the disciples of Jesus are a community that "possesses no inherent right of its own to protect its members in the world, nor do they claim such rights, for they are meek, they renounce every right of their own and live for the sake of Jesus Christ."

They are determined to leave their rights to God alone and so, in faith, they patiently endure. It takes greater strength to trust God for our defense than it does for us to rush to our own defense, but this is the shift to kingdom thinking Jesus requires. It takes more strength to conquer in love than it does to use force or violence.

And Bonhoeffer notes our inheritance is right before us because we have the church, brothers and sisters in Christ, who provide for us in ways money never could.

It is Jesus who prompts you to open your home for the night to a stranger who simply comes in the name of Christ.

It is Jesus who provides you with food in a foreign land, based on nothing more than your testimony that Jesus lives in your heart.

When we answer the call of Christ, we cease to be strangers to all others who have also answered his call.

DAY 44

A Desire for What God Requires

*Blessed are those who hunger and thirst
for righteousness, for they will be filled.*

—MATTHEW 5:6

"Not only do the followers of Jesus
renounce their rights . . . they get no praise
for their achievements or sacrifices."

—DIETRICH BONHOEFFER

Jesus calls us to be aware of the end times coming soon. As disciples of Jesus, we are called to help him bring as many people as possible into the kingdom, and that means we don't have time to stop and argue about our rights and possessions.

We don't allow our rights to distract us from following Jesus. We keep doing what Jesus has told us to do and trust he will take care of the rest. We know nothing will be fully sorted out and made right until the end, so why waste our time protecting temporary positions and possessions that will keep changing until we see the return of Jesus?

Instead, our greatest desire becomes to do what God requires, to "hunger and thirst for righteousness (Matthew 5:6). Bonhoeffer notes we "cannot have righteousness except by hungering and thirsting for it." We develop a longing for the time when all sins will cease and all sins will be forgiven, a time when our transformation will be complete and God's law will be established fully in our hearts.

To follow Jesus means we grow hungry and thirsty *for his righteousness* because we are no longer nourished by our own attempts at righteousness. We realize the futility of preparing such a meal.

Instead, we are nourished only on the righteousness of Christ.

DAY 45

Grace Is Powerfully Other-focused

Don't you see that you can't live however you please,
squandering what God paid such a high price for?

—1 CORINTHIANS 6:19B (MSG)

His life on earth is not finished yet, for he
continues to live in the lives of his followers.

—DIETRICH BONHOEFFER

It's a classic Christian paradox, isn't it? Just when you
think it's time to pull out the law and read someone
the riot act, Jesus shows us that it's better to embrace that
person with a costly love.

And godly grace *does* cost. It clearly cost the Son of God
everything, and for you to extend grace to others will cost
you. Bonhoeffer notes, "For God is a God who bears. The
Son of God bore our flesh, he bore the cross, he bore our
sins, thus making atonement for us. In the same way his
followers are also called upon to bear, and that is precisely
what it means to be a Christian."

In fact, one way to distinguish the difference between
grace and mercy is that grace costs while mercy does not.

Mercy says, "I won't press charges."

Grace says, "I not only won't press charges, I'll pay for your rehab program."

Grace is powerfully other-focused. It gives without fear of depletion. Love, forgiveness, and mercy are handed out with no thought of exhausting the supply.

How would you live differently if you believed you had an inexhaustible supply of God's grace?

DAY 46

Risking Your Reputation

Blessed are the merciful, for they will be shown mercy.
—MATTHEW 5:7

"If any man falls into disgrace, the merciful
will sacrifice their own honour to shield
him, and take his shame upon themselves."
—DIETRICH BONHOEFFER

Bonhoeffer says mercy means we risk our own
reputations as we take on "the distress and humiliation and sin of others." Jesus fills us with "an irresistible love for the down-trodden, the sick, the wretched, the wronged, the outcast and all who are tortured with anxiety."

This is the kind of love that takes on the shame of others in order to bring them into the kingdom of heaven. We may damage our own dignity and honor as we show mercy to publicans and sinners, but that is because we are following Jesus, a man of no reputation.

He calls us be like him. He calls us to reflect the kingdom of heaven, where none of us will be outcasts and we will be covered and protected for all time by the eternal presence of God.

Consider whether you exhibit more loyalty to your reputation or to following Jesus to wherever and whomever he leads.

DAY 47

Be Absorbed by God, Not Your Own Intentions

Happy are the pure in heart, for they will see God.

—MATTHEW 5:8

"Who is pure in heart? . . . Only those
whose hearts are undefiled by their own
evil—and by their own virtues too."

—DIETRICH BONHOEFFER

Jesus says that when our hearts are pure, God will become real to us. Bonhoeffer says this means those "whose hearts are undefiled by their own evil—and by their own virtues too."

This is a critical concept to grasp as we journey into the kingdom of heaven: our own virtue can keep us from fully surrendering to Jesus. We have to abandon the image of the nice guy or girl that we hold in our heads as the images of good Christians.

These images are fantasies that keep us from becoming the image of Christ. Instead of submitting to Jesus, allowing his character to emerge from within us, we'll keep trying to impress or please others with our niceness. We keep submitting to a false image of who we are.

With a pure heart, we become absorbed in God, not our own intentions, "even the purity of high intentions," says Bonhoeffer.

God becomes real to us as we remember we are created in his image and as we follow after Jesus, allowing God's only begotten son to transform us into his image.

DAY 48

Learning to Cooperate with God

Happy are those who work for peace; God
will call them his children! Blessed are the
peacemakers, for they will be called sons of God.

—Matthew 5:9

"The followers of Jesus have been called
to peace. When he called them they
found their peace, for he is their peace."

—Dietrich Bonhoeffer

The peace of Jesus transcends our understanding. It is a peace based on our confidence in God's Word; forged in his forgiveness and strengthened by the heart of a Father. Jesus goes before us, guiding us down the path of peace through the narrow gate into the kingdom of heaven (Phil. 4:7; Luke 1:79; Prov. 3:5–6).

But Bonhoeffer notes the disciples are also called to work for peace, enduring suffering rather than inflicting it and maintaining fellowship when others might break it off. We're called to help others make peace with God, and then help them make peace with each other.

We do this by entering their lives with divine love flowing through us in the same way that Jesus entered our lives: with an aggressive love that would not stop until we made peace with the Father.

"You're blessed when you can show people how to cooperate instead of compete or fight. That's when you discover who you really are, and your place in God's family" (Matt. 5:9 MSG).

DAY 49

Not Recognition, but Rejection

*Blessed are those who are persecuted because of
righteousness, for theirs is the kingdom of heaven.*

—MATTHEW 5:10

"Not recognition, but rejection, is the
reward [the disciples] get from the
world for their message and works."

—DIETRICH BONHOEFFER

Jesus says his disciples will be required to do what is
right and this means we will be persecuted. Bonhoeffer
notes that the blessing for those who are persecuted is the
same as the blessing for humility, perhaps a reminder that
we must wait upon God's justice even when we are faced
with persecution for doing the things God requires of us.

Bonhoeffer says suffering and persecution are requirements of our faith and one of the ways God makes us
Christ-like. "The curse, the deadly persecution and evil
slander confirm the blessed state of the disciples in their
fellowship with Jesus," says Bonhoeffer.

Jesus calls the disciples into a community of believers, where Bonhoeffer says, "the poorest, meekest, and most sorely tried of all men is to be found—on the cross at Golgotha."

We are a community huddle beneath the cross. With Jesus we lose it all, but with Jesus we find it all; he is the resurrection and the life (John 11:25).

If we want to live a godly life, we will be persecuted. This is part of the cost of discipleship. But as we are persecuted, we have the opportunity to trust Jesus, God's Word. We shift from fallen thinking to kingdom thinking when we focus on the promise and not the persecution.

DAY 50

Supernatural Saltiness Flows Through You

You are like salt for the whole human race. But if salt loses its saltiness, there is no way to make it salty again. It has become worthless, so it is thrown out and people trample on it. You are the salt of the earth. But if the salt loses its saltiness, how can it be made salty again? It is no longer good for anything, except to be thrown out and trampled by men.

—MATTHEW 5:13

"The call of Jesus Christ means either that we are the salt of the earth . . . or we are crushed beneath it."

—DIETRICH BONHOEFFER

Jesus says you are salt, a preservative in a world being spoiled by sin. You are salt because you are connected to Jesus and his presence in you slows down the death and decay that contaminates our planet.

Bonhoeffer notes Jesus doesn't say you have the potential to become a salty influence. If you are his disciple, then you are influential. He doesn't say you will eventually become influential. When you follow Jesus, his life immediately begins to flow out of you, creating a contrast with anyone still living for this kingdom of death. You are influential now.

We hear about horrible things happening every day: senseless shootings, suicide bombings, kidnappings, ethnic cleansing, racism, rapes, mass murder by the guy who seemed so quiet to his neighbors.

The wonder is not that it happens; the real wonder is that it doesn't happen more often. Only the hand of God holds back the total collapse of the world, and he uses the supernatural saltiness flowing through you as a divine preservative to hold back the collapse.

Knowing you are the salt of the earth doesn't require you to try harder at being salty. Your saltiness comes from Jesus, not your own efforts. If that is true, where should your focus be? Rather than trying harder to be a preservative, trust Jesus and his declaration that you are salt. Focus on him and he will give you influence.

DAY 51

Re-creating Us as Light

You are the light of the world.
A city on a hill cannot be hidden.
—MATTHEW 5:14

"How impossible, how utterly absurd it would be for
the disciples—these disciples, such men as these!—to
try and become the light of the world! No, they are
already the light, and the call has made them so."
—DIETRICH BONHOEFFER

You are the light of the world. "For God, who said,
'Let light shine out of darkness,' made his light
shine in our hearts to give us the light of the knowledge
of God's glory displayed in the face of Christ" (2 Cor.
4:6 TNIV).

When God formed the world, he said, "Let there be
light!" and there was light. Now he speaks the light of
Jesus into our hearts, and his light shines so powerfully
through us that we are like stars in the universe that point
the whole human race toward real life (Phil. 2:15–16).

This is a portrait of discipleship. Jesus, who is the light of the world, re-creates us into lights within the world. We become light, not because of anything we do ourselves, but because we are in a supernatural union with the Jesus, the Morningstar, the Light of the World.

"Whoever follows me will never walk in darkness, but will have the light of life" (John 8:12 TNIV).

How would your life change if you believed you had the authority of light within your life? You do. What are you going to do now?

DAY 52

No One Lights a Lamp

*Neither do people light a lamp and put it
under a bowl. Instead they put it on its stand,
and it gives light to everyone in the house.*

—MATTHEW 5:15

"The same Jesus who, speaking of himself, said, 'I am the
light,' says to his followers: 'You are the light in your whole
existence, provided you remain faithful to your calling.'"

—DIETRICH BONHOEFFER

When Jesus is present in your life, you cannot be
anything but light. You are not a light for Jesus
because of your spiritual maturity or intellectual enlightenment. His presence creates the light. You are light only
because you are in union with the Light of the World.

To be a disciple means you have no option other than
visibility. You cannot hide or downplay your connection
with Jesus and, if you try, it wouldn't be unfair for others
to wonder about your relationship with Christ.

Bonhoeffer says this is true for the church: "A community of Jesus which seeks to hide itself has ceased to follow him." And this is also true for the individual. If we try to disappear or go unnoticed or "hide our light under a bushel," we deny the call of Jesus on our lives.

It doesn't matter why we try to hide our connection to Jesus; he simply says we can't. When we downplay the Light within us in order to get a promotion or to be acceptable to our friends, we deny the power of Jesus in our life because we are saying that our ability to hide the light has the greater ability to provide for us. We show our unbelief because we place our own agendas and our own loyalties above Jesus.

Do you want the presence of Jesus in your life? If the answer is yes, then you must accept the cost of standing with Jesus in the light, no matter how tempting the shadows may seem. It is a sign of cheap grace when we want the privilege of salvation without the responsibility of sanctified living. See your discipleship as a trust and not a matter of expediency and you will be less likely to compromise. Do you trust the Word of God or not?

DAY 53

Credit God for Our Good Works

*In the same way, let your light shine before men, that they
may see your good deeds and praise your Father in heaven.*

—MATTHEW 5:16

> "It is by seeing the cross and the community
> beneath it that men come to believe in God.
> But that is the light of the Resurrection."

—DIETRICH BONHOEFFER

Jesus does not declare us light in order for us to legislate
morality. We are not declared light so we can set a
good example. We become light because our spirits have
been illuminated by the extraordinary, piercing light of
the cross. That light has its own agenda, and our duty is
simply to obey the command of the one who is the Light
of the World.

We are to let our light shine so that others can see our
good works, but those good works are not good in and of
themselves. They are the result of the light shining into
the darkness. They are not works we create ourselves.
Bonhoeffer says, "these works are none other than those

which the Lord Jesus himself has created in them by calling them to be the light of the world under the shadow of his cross." Paul wrote that we are "created in Christ Jesus to do good works, which God prepared in advance for us to do" (Eph. 2:10).

Our good works do not generate the light. The cross alone illuminates the good works. Our good works do not reveal God; Jesus simply said others will see our good works and glorify God as a result. What becomes visible, Bonhoeffer says, are "the cross and the works of the cross, the poverty and renunciation of the blessed in the beatitudes."

If our good works were the source of the light, that could only be because we are virtuous—and we are decidedly not virtuous. If our virtue were the light that shines into the darkness, then we would deserve the glory, not God.

But our light is meant to shine before people, so they will see our good works and *praise our Father in heaven*. This means the light calls us to an authenticity and humility that points to our Father in heaven. The idea is for us to become less aware that we are light so that we can become more aware of the life of Christ that brings us light (John 1:4-5). In other words, don't fret over how you can be the light in your environment (home, work, school); concentrate on Jesus, who is the Resurrection and the Light, and he will create you as light in your environment.

DAY 54

At Least I Haven't Murdered Anyone

I'm telling you that anyone who is so much as
angry with a brother or sister is guilty of murder. . . .
The simple moral fact is that words kill.

—Matthew 5:22 (MSG)

"Not just the fact that I am angry, but the fact that
there is somebody who has been hurt, damaged
and disgraced by me, who 'has a cause against
me,' erects a barrier between me and God."

—Dietrich Bonhoeffer

God never intended for us to live under the law;
he designed us to live in communion with him.
Because our sin broke that communion, God gave us the
law, starting with Ten Commandments, to push us toward
holy living.

But the law was never meant to be the means for bringing us back to community with God. It was meant to be a
school of Christ, says the Apostle Paul, to teach us not only
the holy ways of God but also the impossibility of meeting
those human standards apart from divine help. God gave

us the law so we would realize how much we need him; so we could learn just how dependent we are upon his grace because we cannot get back to him on our own.

Jesus calls us to follow him into an extraordinary life, a life spent in pursuit of the things that matter to him; a life lived inside the borders of the kingdom of heaven.

Jesus offers no compromise to those who insist on following the law instead of him. He makes it clear that the law demands perfection, and if that isn't enough to topple our arrogance, he explains how perfection is interpreted in the kingdom of heaven. The law says do not commit murder, but understand that includes character assassination. If you've so much as whispered an insult against another person, then you have committed murder. You have already lost your chance to earn your way into the kingdom of heaven.

Most people would assume they can at least make the cut when it comes to murder, thinking, "I mean, at least I haven't murdered anyone." But Jesus knows that the "tongue has the power of life and death . . ." (Prov. 18:21a).

Jesus says the motivations of the heart are more important than appearance. When our motive is to hurt, destroy, or exclude others, we share the same motive with one who murders.

What will Jesus find when he looks into your heart? Don't run from him, run to him, and seek forgiveness for any wrong attitudes.

DAY 55

Desire Must Be Welded to Love

But I tell you that anyone who looks at a woman lustfully
has already committed adultery with her in her heart.

—MATTHEW 5:28

"To follow Jesus means self-renunciation and absolute
adherence to him, and therefore a will dominated
by lust can never be allowed to do what it likes."

—DIETRICH BONHOEFFER

Lust shows a lack of faith. We sell "our heavenly
birthright for a mess of pottage," says Bonhoeffer,
trading off the promises of God for something startlingly
insignificant. "The gains of lust are trivial compared with
the loss it brings—you forfeit your body eternally for the
momentary pleasure of eye or hand," says Bonhoeffer.

The only appropriate place to give our desires free rein
is within the context of godly love, where we look to the
best interests of others and where we see each individual
as a child of God, created to carry the Christ-Spirit.

Lust reveals we're distant from Jesus. Consider how
hard it is to lust after someone while holding Christ in

your thoughts. Try praying for the one you lust for and see how quickly the prayer or the lust wins out: it will be one or the other because you cannot serve two masters. "When you have made your eye the instrument of impurity, you cannot see God with it," says Bonhoeffer.

Yet, Bonhoeffer notes, Jesus is not unreasonable or impractical in his prohibitions. He doesn't forbid them from looking at anything; rather, he says his disciples should look to him. "If they do that he knows that their gaze will always be pure, even when they look upon a woman," Bonhoeffer says.

DAY 56

Grace and Obedience Are Inseparable

From that time on Jesus began to explain to his disciples that he must go to Jerusalem and suffer many things at the hands of the elders, chief priests and teachers of the law, and that he must be killed and on the third Day be raised to life.

—MATTHEW 16:21

"[Jesus] has in fact nothing to add to the commandments of God, except this, that he keeps them."

—DIETRICH BONHOEFFER

Grace in no way frees us from the pursuit of holiness. In truth, grace is given to us to make holy living possible. Imagine holy living as a high wire that you must walk across. One slip and you tumble, forever lost, into the chasm below. But now Jesus stretches a safety net across the chasm. When you slip, you fall into the safety net of grace, acknowledge your mistake, and climb back on the high wire—all the while with Jesus helping and supporting you.

Walking across the chasm on the high wire is now a perfectly reasonable request. If you try to walk across while constantly afraid of slipping, then you are living like a legalist—and you deny the grace of Jesus.

On the other hand, if you try to walk across but you have a cavalier attitude about your steps, even doing things that cause you to fall off the high wire, then you've embraced the concept of cheap grace.

But what Jesus provides is a *net of costly grace*. He keeps us from falling forever into the chasm, but we must follow him by taking the exact steps he tells us to take.

Grace and obedience are not two separate issues; they are bound together in such a way that you cannot claim to be under grace while demanding freedom from obedience.

The reality of freedom—true freedom from the slavery of sin and the entanglements of our impulses—is found in God's grace, but that is not the same as rejecting obedience (Rom. 6:14). "It is for freedom that Christ has set us free. Stand firm, then, and do not let yourselves be burdened again by a yoke of slavery" (Gal. 5:1).

Resting in God's grace will make you want to do what is required. If you struggle with obedience, turn first to Jesus before you follow any lists such as "Five Steps to Greater Obedience." It is in intimacy with Jesus that you find your freedom, and he will create in you a desire to follow his commands.

DAY 57

Follow Jesus, not Lists

*For I tell you that unless your righteousness surpasses
that of the Pharisees and the teachers of the law,
you will certainly not enter the kingdom of heaven.*

—MATTHEW 5:20

"[Discipleship to Jesus] means that adherence
to the law is something quite different from the
following of Christ, and, secondly, it means that
any adherence to his person that disregards the
law is equally removed from the following of him."

—DIETRICH BONHOEFFER

Instead of following Jesus, we follow our lists.

But the problem with lists is that you not only have
to accomplish everything on the list perfectly, but just
having the list gives you a false sense of security. It causes
you to lose sight of the other parts of the law, the smallest
details, that you failed to place on the list. When we fail to
plan to follow the law completely, as the saying goes, we
plan to fail.

When Jesus says he requires a more faithful pursuit of the law, he doesn't mean at all that we are capable of fulfilling every jot and tittle ourselves. Rather, he means we must live by faith in him, not by lists. We must live not by an independence born of cheap grace, but by the obedience that leads to belief in him.

Bonhoeffer says you can adhere to the law religiously and not be a follower of Jesus Christ, but if you follow Jesus, you cannot disregard the law. You may not be able to fulfill the law, but you cannot disregard it. Jesus fulfills it for you, and his bloody gift of doing so is far removed from any fantasies of cheap grace.

When we follow Jesus, we enter into a union with Jesus that allows us to share in a righteousness that is better than the Pharisees. This shouldn't give us a superior attitude; we've done nothing to earn our righteousness.

Instead, we should act justly, love mercy, and walk humbly with our God (Mic. 6:8).

DAY 58

It Takes Faith to Be Faithful

*Those who belong to Christ Jesus have crucified the
sinful nature with its passions and desires. Since we
live by the Spirit, let us keep in step with the Spirit.*

—GALATIANS 5:24–25

"Lust is impure because it is unbelief,
and therefore it is to be shunned."

—DIETRICH BONHOEFFER

Jesus knows you're fighting against natural instincts,
and he's not insensitive to your plight. He was human;
he struggled with the same temptations you do. Is he
telling you to get tough and defeat this lust issue on
your own?

Actually, no. He knows you can't do it on your own.
Instead of fighting against your basic instincts, Jesus
wants you to step into his grace—the costly grace Jesus
died to give you as a free gift. Jesus went to the cross to pay
for your sin of lust, but he rose from the dead to give you
new life, a new way to confront the sin of lust.

Jesus wants to replace your instinct with the Holy Spirit so that, instead of being a slave to impulse, you are free to make pure choices when it comes to lust and sex. Through the Holy Spirit, you have the power of the divine nature working inside you. You access that power through faith—believing the Spirit is there and at work to help you overcome the sin of lust.

When you are tempted, you have a choice: do you believe fulfilling your lust is best for you, or do you believe that the reason Jesus condemns lust is because he knows it will keep you from becoming all that you can be? Will you believe Jesus, or your impulses?

The Apostle Paul says, "It is God's will that you should be sanctified: that you should avoid sexual immorality; that each of you should learn to control his own body in a way that is holy and honorable, not in passionate lust like the heathen, who do not know God . . . For God did not call us to be impure, but to live a holy life. Therefore, he who rejects this instruction does not reject man but God, who gives you his Holy Spirit" (1 Thess. 4:3–5, 7–8).

See your lust as unbelief and you will be less likely to give in to temptation. Instead of trying harder to fight temptation, trust God to provide for your every need. Sexual desire is natural to being human. God will either provide for your need in a legitimate way (through marriage) or he will give you the grace to live in abstinence. The grace is there: will you accept it or reject it?

DAY 59

Our Despair Prepares Us for Grace

*"Woe to me!" I cried. "I am ruined! For I am a man of
unclean lips, and I live among a people of unclean lips,
and my eyes have seen the King, the LORD Almighty."*

—Isaiah 6:5

"In this question of truthfulness, what matters
first and last is that a man's whole being should be
exposed, his whole evil laid bare in the sight of God."

—Dietrich Bonhoeffer

Despite his impeccable integrity, the prophet Isaiah
was overwhelmed with the unholiness of his life
when brought before the truth. He saw his need for grace
and cried, "Woe to me! . . . I am ruined!" (Isa. 6:5).

Yet, Isaiah's story shows that Jesus never intends to
leave us in despair (Rom. 7:24–25). His intent is to pre-
pare us to receive God's grace. Even as Isaiah is staggered
by the revelation of his sin, he just as suddenly finds himself cleansed of his guilt and forgiven of his sins when he
is touched by a burning coal from heaven's altar (Isa. 6:7).

He is then energized for God's purpose: "Then I heard the voice of the Lord saying, 'Whom shall I send? And who will go for us?' And I said, 'Here am I. Send me!" (Isa. 6:8).

In the same way, our call to discipleship cleanses us and energizes us to follow Jesus. But we have to face the truth about ourselves, or the lie will constantly undermine our ability to follow Jesus.

The cross is God's truth about us and anything we do to sidestep this truth simply leaves us in a lie. If we could reach God's standard of truth on our own, if we could fulfill the requirements of the law, then Christ died for nothing (Gal. 2:21).

Our self-righteousness is nothing less than an arrogant assault upon the holiness of God, and when we wink at our sin—any sin—we cheapen the price that Jesus paid to cleanse us from those sins.

Jesus shows us our sin, not to condemn us, but to create in us a desire to come to him to be cleansed of all unrighteousness. Do you believe Jesus comes in compassion? If so, why would you fear confessing your sins before him?

DAY 60

The Whole Truth on Display

We refuse to wear masks and play games. We don't
maneuver and manipulate behind the scenes. And
we don't twist God's Word to suit ourselves. Rather,
we keep everything we do and say out in the open, the
whole truth on display, so that those who want to can
see and judge for themselves in the presence of God.

—2 CORINTHIANS 4:2 (MSG)

"If the world refuses justice, the Christian will pursue
mercy, and if the world takes refuge in lies, he will open
his mouth for the dumb, and bear testimony to the truth."

—DIETRICH BONHOEFFER

When we try to separate truth from grace, we end
up crucifying the Truth, Jesus, God's Own Son,
because we're unwilling to crucify the self. Instead, we
keep trying to live by lists that nurture the lie that we're
living up to God's standard of holiness. The rules were
never meant to replace the relationship.

On the other hand, when we try to separate grace from
truth, we not only sacrifice truth, we abandon the sacrifice
and passion of Jesus. Instead, we cling to the lie that grace

is all about getting along and going along. Grace is free, but it is costly in that we must live from now on in the Truth.

The fact is we cannot have true, authentic Christian community without truth because our relationship with Jesus, the Truth, effects the truthfulness and transparency of our relationship with all others.

It is only in this transparent community that we can see each other as we truly are, where we can grow up in Christ, speaking the truth in love as iron sharpens iron. In such a truth community, there is no need to "read between the lines or look for hidden meanings" because we speak "a plain, unembellished truth . . ." (2 Cor. 1:13 MSG).

We need not fear exposure because everything is already out in the open, and everyone in the community is committed to speaking the truth, living the truth, and following the truth no matter where it leads.

A utopia? Certainly not by the standards of Jesus, the truth incarnate. Impossible? Absolutely, if we try to create such a community independent of the truth incarnate.

And this is our constant challenge: Will we try to define truth separate from God's standard? Will we try to live independent of the one who is the Truth? Will we ignore the truth and live a lie?

We cannot answer these questions once and consider the matter settled. We answer them throughout the day, every day, as we make decisions, both large and small, regarding how far we will follow the truth.

DAY 61

When We Hide the Truth, It Is a Faith Issue

*A man with leprosy came and knelt before him and said,
"Lord, if you are willing, you can make me clean." Jesus
reached out his hand and touched the man. "I am willing,"
he said. "Be clean!" Immediately he was cured of his leprosy.*

—MATTHEW 8:2–3

"The cross is God's truth about us, and therefore
it is the only power which can make us truthful."

—DIETRICH BONHEOFFER

When we hide the truth, it is a faith issue; not a
circumstance issue.

It takes faith to be truthful. It takes faith to come clean.
It takes faith to be authentic and transparent in our
relationships. It takes faith to stop pretending and to let
others see who we really are and what we're really about.

Praise God, we have Jesus, our mediator. Even if we
sin, we need not live in fear because he sits at the right
hand of the Father as our advocate. He understands our
weaknesses; he was tempted in "in every way, just as

we are—yet was without sin. Let us then approach the throne of grace with confidence, so that we may receive mercy and find grace to help us in our time of need" (Heb. 4:15–16).

The point is, Jesus wants to cleanse us, not condemn us. Jesus came to do whatever was necessary to cleanse us of our sins so that we could come home to the Father. Again and again, we see Jesus in the New Testament willing to use his power to heal; we see him willing to use his authority to cleanse.

This is why, when we hide the truth, it is a faith issue. We place more faith in manipulating circumstances or our ability to hide the truth than we do in Jesus to be compassionate and caring.

The thing is not to try harder, particularly if our trying involves hiding or manipulating the truth. The thing is to trust more when Jesus says, in effect, "I do want to make you clean and whole, and I can do it. Come to me and I'll teach you to walk fully in grace and truth."

We trust that Jesus means what he says and we step into his Truth. What lie or hypocrisy are you hiding that comes to mind right now? Jesus wants to embrace you with his truth. Confess it as you hand it to him in obedient trust.

DAY 62

We Are Character Witnesses

On the other hand, whoever obeys the Law and teaches
others to do the same, will be great in the Kingdom of heaven.
Anyone who breaks one of the least of these commandments
and teaches others to do the same will be called least in the
kingdom of heaven, but whoever practices and teaches these
commands will be called great in the kingdom of heaven.

—MATTHEW 5:19

"And since you are that light, you can no
longer remain hidden, even if you want to."

—DIETRICH BONHOEFFER

In the school of Christ, the curriculum is Christ—we
are to learn Christ (Eph. 4:20).

Yet, Jesus is also the Teacher—we need to hear him
(Eph. 4:21). The way we learn who Jesus is and what he
is up to in our lives is from him. And the only way to
learn from him is to follow him in obedience to his word.
Through our obedience—our adherence to him—we
become like him, but we also find out who we are and why
God created us.

Jesus says our discipleship isn't just about being obedient; we must teach others to do the same. The disciples of Jesus, then, are basically character witnesses. When life calls us to testify as to what is right or wrong, true or false, we bear witness "in whatever we do in word or in deed" to the nature of our Lord (Col. 3:17).

Always and in all ways, we make it our aim to "tell others about Christ, warning everyone and teaching everyone with all the wisdom God has given us. We want to present them to God, perfect in their relationship to Christ" (Col. 1:28 NLT). When we try to do this apart from Jesus, we will find ourselves drowning in spiritual information but unable to navigate the waters of transformation. Maybe this is why we have so much religious education yet so little spiritual formation.

Instead of a genuine devotion to "say something special from God" and, therefore, ". . . learn from each other" (1 Cor. 14:30-31, MSG), we try to teach and counsel with words we've picked up second-hand from others. Our goal is not just to know the word, but to know Jesus as the Word.

Our focus is on Jesus, not how much we know, not what someone else said. We learn from Jesus and then we point others to Jesus. This is a part of the natural rhythm of grace—and why it is so important to remain intimate with Jesus. Ask Jesus to show you the most important thing you can do each day to remain intimate with him.

DAY 63

The Right to Revenge

But I tell you, Do not resist an evil person.

—MATTHEW 5:39A

"At this point it becomes evident that when a
Christian meets with injustice, he no longer
clings to his rights and defends them at all costs."

—DIETRICH BONHOEFFER

If you want to follow Jesus, then you must give up
your right to take revenge. Jesus places before you the
choice of trusting God to handle the situation or trusting
your own abilities. The choice you make reveals where you
place your faith.

Bonhoeffer notes that the Old Testament established
a system of retribution—"an eye for an eye"—but Jesus,
again, pushes his disciples to the greater righteousness
required in the kingdom of heaven (Matt. 5:20).

Think of it like this: You can live in this world and live
according to the law, or you can enter into the kingdom
of heaven, subjecting yourself to the standards of grace.
If you live according to the law, you will fail. In truth,

you already have. If you follow Jesus into the kingdom of heaven, he will handle the details of the law for you and he will also energize you to live by the higher standard he demands.

Jesus is not repudiating the Old Testament law of retribution, Bonhoeffer writes. He came to fulfill the law, not abolish it (Matt. 5:17). What Jesus is doing is pushing his disciples into the redemptive realm of grace, where we trust God to defend us and we trust God to redeem us.

And we trust that God knows what to do with our enemies, even if that means he redeems them, too.

Would you rather God condemn your enemies or redeem them?

DAY 64

Jesus Never Ignored Evil

The weapons we fight with are not the weapons of the
world. On the contrary, they have divine power to demolish
strongholds. We demolish arguments and every pretension
that sets itself up against the knowledge of God, and we
take captive every thought to make it obedient to Christ.

—2 CORINTHIANS 10:4–5

"Surely we do not wish to accuse Jesus of ignoring
the reality and power of evil! Why, the whole
of his life was one long conflict with the devil."

—DIETRICH BONHOEFFER

Since God is working on retribution, we can stop
fighting like creatures that have been abandoned by
their Creator, as if our only choice is to deploy weapons of
revenge, such as manipulation, blame, shame, hatred, bitterness, pride, gossip, slander, ridicule, threats, deception, violence in anger, and violence with cold-blooded calculation.

These are satanic weapons we use to get our own way
without the help of God (2 Cor. 10:4–5). They just keep us
in a cycle of evil-for-evil. Jesus came to end that cycle.

Bonhoeffer says disciples should resist evil in the same way Jesus did on his way to the cross. "Suffering willingly endured is stronger than evil, it spells death to evil," he writes. "The worse the evil, the readier must the Christian be to suffer; he must let the evil person fall into Jesus' hands."

Bonhoeffer also notes that Jesus is not naive about evil. He knows evil first-hand, and he is not referring to some esoteric evil in the abstract. He is pushing us to confront evil with faith, looking past the evil-doer and the evil act to see God still in control.

When we suffer willingly, we hand our enemies over to Jesus—that is, they are no longer resisting us; they are resisting Jesus. Jesus calls us to respond to evil with belief in his promises; that is, we look past evil into the loving eyes of the Father, where we can see he is at work responding to the ways we've been wronged.

Why would you want to take retribution into your own hands instead of trusting the God of the universe to handle it?

DAY 65

Redemption, Not Retribution

But I tell you, Do not resist an evil person. If someone
strikes you on the right cheek, turn to him the other also.

—Matthew 5:39

"And the cross is the only justification for the precept of
non-violence, for it alone can kindle a faith in the victory
over evil which will enable men to obey that precept."

—Dietrich Bonhoeffer

When Jesus hung on the Cross, he showed us how
to handle revenge.

He would not allow anyone or any circumstance to
divert him from his objective to love each and every one
of us into the kingdom of heaven and into the presence
of God. He remained committed to doing only what the
Father told him to do, trusting that God would handle any
need for vengeance.

If Jesus had stopped to seek revenge against those who
had wronged him, he would have been distracted from his
holy mission. The truth is, he would have undermined the
very thing that the Father sent him to do.

Jesus is on a mission of redemption, not retribution.

God has the better perspective. He knows why things happened and what was intended. He knows who's wronged you. He says there will be a vengeance day, but keep in mind God also knows whom you have wronged and who is seeking vengeance against you (Luke 21)! He knows who needs to be punished on that day for hurting you, and he also know what punishment you should receive on that day for the way you have hurt others.

When we take the path of Jonah, insisting that God rain fire down upon our enemies, we are rebelling against the sovereignty of God, who has the right to decide who should be blessed and who should be banished. When we demand an eye for an eye, Jesus holds out his hand without demanding a nail for a nail.

The blood of Jesus "speaks of forgiveness instead of crying out for vengeance like the blood of Abel" (Heb. 12:24 NLT). The cross shows us how Jesus handled revenge. When you think of Jesus, do you think of him as taking revenge upon those who hurt him?

DAY 66

No More Tit-for-Tat

*Here's what I propose: "Don't hit back at all." If someone
strikes you, stand there and take it. If someone drags you
into court and sues for the shirt off your back, giftwrap
your best coat and make a present of it. And if someone
takes unfair advantage of you, use the occasion to practice
the servant life. No more tit-for-tat stuff. Live generously.*

—MATTHEW 5:39–42 (MSG)

"When a man unjustly demands that I should
give him my coat, I offer him my cloak also, and
so counter his demand; when he requires me to
go the other mile, I go willingly, and show up
his exploitation of my service for what it is."

—DIETRICH BONHOEFFER

Jesus says in the kingdom of heaven your focus is no
longer on yourself but on others.

• When someone tries to humiliate you, Jesus says
confront him with your humility.

- When someone tries to take what is yours, Jesus says confront her by giving even more.
- Instead of demanding security, Jesus says we should voluntarily give away the things we normally hold back to protect us in the future.
- Instead of demanding freedom, Jesus says we should voluntarily carry the burdens of others.

In a sense, Jesus is saying, "I have better things for you to do than to chase after revenge. I want you focused on kingdom work, helping me to bring others into the kingdom. So don't be foolish! Revenge is a job that our Father set aside for himself. Do you really think you can do a better job than God at getting even? Do you really want to get in the way of God when he is handling revenge for you?"

It is the kind of faith David showed when he approached Goliath, saying, "You come against me with sword and spear and javelin, but I come against you in the name of the Lord Almighty, the God of the armies of Israel, whom you have defied" (1 Sam. 17:45).

It is the kind of trust in Jesus you will be challenged to show the next time someone wrongs you or unjustly demands something from you.

DAY 67

Love Defined in Uncompromising Terms

But I tell you: Love your enemies and
pray for those who persecute you.

—MATTHEW 5:44

"Had Jesus only told us to love our brethren, we
might have misunderstood what he meant by
love, but [in saying we're to love our enemies] he
leaves us in no doubt whatever as to his meaning."

—DIETRICH BONHOEFFER

Jesus is absolutely relentless in pushing the standards of the law to a higher level—in truth, the level at which they've always been in the kingdom of heaven. In this case, he speaks about the law of love, insisting it must be a love that is extraordinary and remarkable.

He calls us, Bonhoeffer notes, to a sacrificial love where we love our enemies in exactly the same way we love our friends. Yet he adds, "By our enemies Jesus means those who are quite intractable and utterly unresponsive to our love, who forgive us nothing when we forgive them all, who requite our love with hatred and our service with derision."

Our enemies may reject our love; they may waste our love, discount our love, and react angrily to our love. They may never understand our love or even be changed through our love; yet, Jesus calls us to love them without these guarantees. In doing this, he is calling us to become more like him: "While we were still sinners, Christ died for us" (Rom. 5:8).

Bonhoeffer notes this is the kind of love that asks nothing in return. It is a love that needs no reason. God doesn't give us his love because of something we've done; he doesn't give us his love because of something he might gain; and he doesn't give us his love because we deserve it.

He just gives his love—because.

DAY 68

Jesus Sets the Standard for Love

If you love those who love you, what reward will
you get? Are not even the tax collectors doing that?

—MATTHEW 5:46

"His behaviour must be determined not by the way others
treat him, but by the treatment he himself receives from
Jesus; it has only one source, and that is the will of Jesus."

—DIETRICH BONHOEFFER

Jesus calls us to a kind of love that "cuts right across
[our] ideas of good and evil," says Bonhoeffer. We love,
not according to the way others love us, but according to
the way Jesus loves us.

Bonhoeffer says Christ calls us to love our enemies with
the same love we would have for a precious lover. "The
Christian must treat his enemy as a brother, and requite
his hostility with love," says Bonhoeffer.

It is a sure sign we are entering the kingdom of heaven
when we begin to see our enemies with the eyes of Jesus,
understanding that God's way to defeat them is by
loving them.

Fallen men and women cannot do this; only those who carry Jesus within and who respond obediently to the commands of Jesus can. Only those who trust in Jesus can love with the love of God flowing through them.

Otherwise, their love is a diminished love that lacks the power to overcome evil, a shadow love that mixes selfish motives—perhaps in the face of an enemy, the motive of self-preservation—with unqualified, godly motives.

Bonhoeffer says Jesus calls us to a love that makes no distinction between one enemy or the other and no distinction between a private enemy or a public one (that is, someone we personally know in contrast to someone, say, in public office whose policies are designed to harm us).

Regardless we are to offer unqualified love to our enemies. We're to bless them, do good for them, and pray for them.

DAY 69

'Love Your Enemies ....'

*I'm challenging that. I'm telling you to love your
enemies. Let them bring out the best in you, not the
worst. When someone gives you a hard time, respond
with the energies of prayer, for then you are working
out of your true selves, your God-created selves.*

MATTHEW 5:44-45A (MSG)

"Love asks nothing in return, but seeks those who need
it. And who needs our love more than those who are
consumed with hatred and are utterly devoid of love?"

—DIETRICH BONHOEFFER

Jesus commands us to an active love of our enemies.
Our love is more than just a passive bearing of persecution and hatred. We must engage in loving our enemies
by blessing them, doing good for them, and praying for
them regardless of who they are or what they have done.

Bonhoeffer says, "We are not to imagine that this is
to condone his evil; such a love proceeds from strength
rather than weakness, from truth rather than fear, and
therefore it cannot be guilty of the hatred of another."

It is a fearless love, where we recognize God loved us even when we were his enemies, and now, by his love within us, we can love our enemies with the same love aimed at redemption.

But do you see how this is related to our faith? When we trust that God is committed to loving the sin and fallenness out of us, we can then, in faith, commit to loving the sin and fallenness out of our enemies. We can obediently let the love of Christ flow through us, driving away the cycle of fear that keeps us locked in hostility with our enemies.

In this way, we are conformed to the image of Christ instead of the image of our enemies (Rom. 12:2).

DAY 70

Real Love Is More Than Mere Theory

My old self has been crucified with Christ.
It is no longer I who live, but Christ lives in me.
So I live in this earthly body by trusting in the
Son of God, who loved me and gave himself for me.

—GALATIANS 2:20 (NLT)

"To confess and testify to the truth as it is in Jesus,
and at the same time to love the enemies of that
truth, his enemies and ours, and to love them with the
infinite love of Jesus Christ, is indeed a narrow way."

—DIETRICH BONHOEFFER

It is profoundly easier to live and to love "philosophically" or in some future tense ("Someday I will") than to do so in the reality of the present moment. For example, you may love the fantasy of a perfect spouse but not actually love your spouse!

It takes no effort to love the dream of your children—what they could be or should be or would be if they'd just listen to you. But genuinely loving the child—the

156

teenage child who's acting like your spouse's side of the family—that's altogether different, isn't it?

God's command to love forces us out of our fantasies, where other people are always accommodating us and adjusting to all of our preferences, and then his command pushes us to learn to love others as he loved us, regardless of performance or appearance.

Real love is more than nice thoughts or feelings. We may not feel like meeting the needs of difficult people. Rather, we feel like pointing out their flaws. We may think a certain person is worth less than our time, attention, or energy, and that tempts us be to devalue their worth in order to avoid dealing with them.

In such moments, Jesus' command to love as he loves comes to bear, and this is how we enter into the reality of genuine community. Our standard should no longer be measured by what feels good or bad.

What is real love, then? It is love rooted in Jesus' love. Jesus is relentless in his command that we "love one another, just as I love you"—which means loving personal and up-close, meeting the needs of the undeserving, not attacking their faults.

This is how we learn by the word "Not I, but Christ" (Gal 2:20): We begin to see it is no longer just "I" doing the loving. In truth, if it is only "I" doing the loving, then we are bound to fail because the divine nature is not at the core of our love.

DAY 71

The God of All that Is Personal

But we come from God and belong to God. Anyone who knows God understands us and listens. The person who has nothing to do with God will, of course, not listen to us. This is another test for telling the Spirit of Truth from the spirit of deception.

—1 JOHN 4:6 (MSG)

"This righteousness is therefore not a duty owed,
but a perfect and truly personal communion with
God, and Jesus not only possesses this righteousness,
but is himself the personal embodiment of it."

—DIETRICH BONHOEFFER

Jesus did not come to us as a religion, a set of laws, nor did he come merely as an ideal—he came in person! Through his death and resurrection, he brings us into the personal embrace of a passionate and loving union. This means we are grafted into the nature of Jesus and "in him we live and move and have our being" (Acts 17:28).

We live in a world where the absence of personal touch is glaring. From email to ATMs to "listen to these options" automatic operators, it seems ever more difficult to connect.

We move in a realm that increasingly views the impersonal as able to save us—acting as though better organization, purer methodology, quicker computation, and acquiring more and newer possessions will somehow deliver us from our meaninglessness and hopelessness.

We expect all this from the world, but we shouldn't tolerate it in the body of Christ. For "we come from God and belong to God" (1 John 4:6 MSG), the Creator and Protector of all that is personal.

We're called to be like Jesus, to personally interact and invest in one another's lives and to do it in a way that is meaningful to the person we serve. Jesus commands us to bind ourselves to each other, caring for one another the way Jesus cares for us.

Through our personalized expressions of love for each other, we anticipate and answer the question, "Do you want to see who the word of God is and how he personally loves us? Watch how we love one another."

DAY 72

Our Love for One Another Must Be Personal

Your love for one another will prove to
the world that you are my disciples.

—JOHN 13:35 (NLT)

"Neighbourliness is not a quality in other people, it is
simply their claim on ourselves. Every moment and every
situation challenges us to action and to obedience."

—DIETRICH BONHOEFFER

We'll never carry out our mission as disciples of
Jesus from behind pulpits or within Bible stud-
ies. Jesus commands that we "go therefore" and fill the
earth with his presence so others may "observe" what he
commanded us—to love one another as he loves us (Matt.
28:19–20; John 13:34). We are to take our unseen and
eternal fellowship, our oneness with him and each other,
into the seen and temporal lives of others.

As others observe us "being of the same mind, maintaining the same love, intent on one purpose; not merely
looking out for our own personal interests, but also for

each other's interests" (Phil 2:3–4), they will naturally wonder where such uncommon attitudes come from.

And we have opportunity to say, "This is the attitude that 'is in Christ Jesus who, although He existed in the form of God, did not regard equality with God as a thing to be grasped (and used for His own interest), but emptied Himself, taking the form of a bond servant, being made in the likeness of men'" (Phil 2:5–7 NAS).

Now he inhabits our likeness for the same purpose. He is filling us with himself so we may empty ourselves of our self-interested concerns and take upon ourselves the interests and concerns of others.

In a fallen and self-oriented world, both that attitude and practice are particularly uncommon and profoundly noticeable. The witness of the reality of Christ and his love through our authentic and loving relationships is a living testimony with which the world must deal. Jesus' personal and sacrificial love creates a safe place, a refuge, an opportunity to "be" that every person needs.

God created us in such a way that we are not fully human until we are connected to Christ. This pulls us into community with Jesus and others. We were never meant to follow Jesus by ourselves. We grow and mature in *community* with other believers, where, Bonhoeffer says, "we are delivered from that individualism which is the consequence of sin."

DAY 73

Set Apart to Become Like Jesus

Those whom God had already chosen he also set apart
to become like his Son, so that the Son would be the first
among many believers. For those God foreknew he also
predestined to be conformed to the likeness of his Son,
that he might be the firstborn among many brothers.

—ROMANS 8:29

"To be called to a life of extraordinary quality, to live up to
it, and yet to be unconscious of it is indeed a narrow way."

—DIETRICH BONHOEFFER

Bonhoeffer says we are called to "a life of extraordinary quality." To be a disciple of Jesus means:

- We are separated from the world—"We are separated
  from the world, not like cloistered monks withdrawn
  from the world, but rather as a people set apart by
  God to become like his son" (Rom. 8:29–30). We are
  in the world, but not of the world, separated from
  others by the Holy Spirit working within us, yet

interacting with others because we are in union with Christ, the mediator between God and fallen man.

- We transcend human standards—The work of Jesus in us transcends our own standards of righteousness and, although he gives his righteousness to us, following him will often lead us to do more than the law requires. We must go the extra mile.

- We live extraordinary lives—We are extraordinary because Christ is working through us. We can no longer live average lives because we are now in union with Jesus; we live with a constant, real connection to God's divine nature.

Bonhoeffer notes there is an obvious temptation to "mistake Christ's work for a commendation of a new, however novel, free and inspiring pattern for pious living. How eagerly would the religious embrace a life of poverty, truthfulness, and suffering, if only they might thereby satisfy their yearning not only to believe, but to see with their own eyes!"

When we demand to see everything with our own eyes, when we demand that we understand each step before we take it, we are no longer living in faith.

Don't Try to Appear Good

*Make certain you do not perform your religious duties
in public so that people will see what you do. If you do
these things publicly, you will not have any reward from
your Father in heaven. Be careful not to do your "acts
of righteousness" before men, to be seen by them. If you
do, you will have no reward from your Father in heaven.*

—MATTHEW 6:1

"If you do good, you must not let your left hand
know what your right hand is doing . . . Otherwise
you are simply displaying your own virtue, and
not that which has its source in Jesus Christ."

—DIETRICH BONHOEFFER

The cost of discipleship is that we must put an end
to our spiritual pride. We must ruthlessly abandon
any attempts to be good or appear good on our own. Our
good deeds must flow from our connection to Jesus and
not the other way around. We bring no goodness to him
and we must reject any thoughts that suggest otherwise.

And because there is a danger we will become impressed with our own piety and service to God, Jesus says we must be visible in our Christian character but invisible in Christian service. "Be especially careful when you are trying to be good so that you don't make a performance out of it," says Jesus. "It might be good theater, but the God who made you won't be applauding" (Matt. 6:1 MSG).

Jesus continues to get us ready for the kingdom of heaven. In a sense, he says once we pass through the narrow gate, we won't think about how we look—good or bad—when we stop to help others. We'll just do it, allowing the love of Jesus to pour spontaneously out of us into the lives of others.

The problem is, when we start thinking about how our service looks or whom it might impress, we've changed the nature of what we're doing. It's no longer an act of love and that means it's no longer noticeable in the kingdom of heaven.

How would your prayers change if you were not trying to impress anyone or concerned about what others thought of you?

DAY 75

Becoming Like Jesus in Prayer

*And when you pray, do not be like the hypocrites,
for they love to pray standing in the synagogues and
on the street corners to be seen by men. I tell you
the truth, they have received their reward in full.*

—MATTHEW 6:5

"True prayer does not depend either on the individual
or the whole body of the faithful . . . That makes
God the sole object of our prayers, and frees us from
a false confidence in our own prayerful efforts."

—DIETRICH BONHOEFFER

Prayer is an intimate conversation with your Heavenly
Father. When you try to impress others with your
ability to pray, you mock that intimacy. You appear to be
focusing on the Father when you're actually focusing on
yourself—your needs, your wants, your ability to persuade
and bully God, and your desire to impress others with
your knowledge of how to get God to give you what you
want when you want it.

It's absolutely no different from standing up and saying, "Look at me so you can be impressed with how connected I am to God!"

Eugene Peterson paraphrases Jesus' comments this way, "The world is full of so-called prayer warriors who are prayer-ignorant. They're full of formulas and programs and advice, peddling techniques for getting what you want from God. Don't fall for that nonsense. This is your Father you are dealing with, and he knows better than you what you need" (Matt. 6:7–8 MSG).

If your motivation in prayer is to impress people, then Jesus says you will get what you want: praise from other people. In truth, that is exactly what you are asking for when you pray to impress: "Give me the praise of others." Jesus indicates God sees no need to reward you for these self-promoting prayers. They represent worldly thinking. Why would God reward you for that, when he wants you to pray like someone who is part of the kingdom of heaven?

Before you start to pray, take a long, deep breath, and think about your Father in heaven. Speak to him and no one else as you pray. How would your prayers be different if you knew God wanted to know you intimately? He does, so ask him to bring you to just such a place of obedient trust.

DAY 76

Christian Prayer Presupposes Faith

*But when you pray, go into your room, close the door
and pray to your Father, who is unseen. Then your
Father, who sees what is done in secret, will reward you.*

—MATTHEW 6:6

"Christian prayer presupposes faith, that is,
adherence to Christ. He is the one and only Mediator
of our prayers. We pray at his command, and
to that word Christian prayer is always bound."

—DIETRICH BONHOEFFER

onhoeffer notes that Jesus is proof that God wants
intimacy with us. He came to create a bridge to God,
and we become intimate with the Father through Jesus.

This is another problem with prayers of pride. They
set us up to be false mediators between others and God.
They slyly say, "Look at how I pray. Watch me and see how
persuasive I can be with God."

They suggest we have a special connection with God
independent of our connection through Christ, and
that encourages others to believe our prayers have more

meaning before God than their prayers—when the gospel truth is, anyone connected to God through Jesus can approach the throne of grace boldly (Heb. 4:16).

Bonhoeffer says, "[Jesus] is the one and only Mediator of our prayers. We pray at his command, and to that word Christian prayer is always bound." This is the reason we pray in the name of Jesus and why eliminating the name of Jesus from our prayers is a significant theological issue.

It is important to note, then, the distinct difference between being an intercessor for others and any arrogant attempt to be a mediator for them. We do not connect anyone to God; Jesus connects them to God. But Jesus calls us to intercede on behalf of others, standing beside and sometimes standing *instead* as we fulfill the law of Christ by taking the burdens of others to God in prayer (Gal. 6:2).

When you pray in the name of Jesus, you can trust that your prayers are heard and that they will be answered. How would your prayers be different if you knew beyond a shadow of a doubt that God will answer them? Ask him to bring you to just such a place of obedient trust.

DAY 77

Peace Be with You

As you enter the home, give it your greeting.
—MATTHEW 10:12

"This is no empty formula, for it immediately brings the power of the peace of God on those who are worthy of it."
—DIETRICH BONHOEFFER

Bonhoeffer notes, as the disciples enter a house during their journey, they're told to use the same word of greeting as Jesus, their Master: "Peace to this house" (Luke 10:5b).

We come representing Jesus. We bring the Good News that Jesus has entered our conflict with God, bringing a ruthless love that will not stop until we have surrendered to God. We bring the Good News that our Savior and Mediator is benevolent in victory, able to say, "Go in peace and be freed from your suffering" (Mark 5:34).

There will be those who will not listen and they will reject us, but in rejecting us, they are actually rejecting Jesus. This is a sign of kingdom thinking growing strong within us—that we can see past the rejection of others into the reality of eternity. It is not our job to plead and beg them into the kingdom. We do not have to make them listen to us or insist they believe the truth.

We are no longer responsible for them, says Jesus, underscoring that he will authorize our efforts and expand or limit our ministry according to his needs, his will, his plan. We are told to stop our own efforts and hand them over to God. We're to shake the dust from our feet and leave them to God's judgment.

Rejection is a risk Jesus is willing to take on his mission for you and he calls us to face rejection in our service to him. When we face rejection, Jesus is not disappointed in us; rather, his grief is with those who refuse to listen: "If you, even you, had only known on this day what would bring you peace—but now it is hidden from your eyes" (Luke 19:42).

Ask God to help you truly believe this: You do not have to force others to listen to you or insist they believe the truth. You simply have to bring them the Good News.

DAY 78

When They Persecute You ...

I am sending you out like sheep among wolves. Therefore
be as shrewd as snakes and as innocent as doves. Be
on your guard against men; they will hand you over
to the local councils and flog you in their synagogues.
On my account you will be brought before governors
and kings as witnesses to them and to the Gentiles.

—MATTHEW 10:16–18

"With this the Lord promises them his
abiding presence . . . Nothing can happen
to them without Jesus knowing of it."

—DIETRICH BONHOEFFER

To suggest the Christian life is a gateway to problem-free, stress-less living is a sign of fallen thinking. Our lives in Christ are meant to be extraordinary, incredible, and purposeful but never trouble-free. We're to step into the will of God and stay there, trusting he has our best interests at heart, even though he tells us that circumstances seem so bad that we doubt his promises (Jer. 29:11, Rom. 8:28, Phil. 4:13).

Rather than taking us out of the problems of life, making us appear amazing to others; he keeps us in the pressure-cooker so others can see how a life connected to Jesus confronts problems in a very different way than a life disconnected from the divine nature. We handle difficult situations differently because we are energized by the Holy Spirit; we respond to hardship like people from the kingdom of heaven, not like people seemingly abandoned by God or in rebellion to God or unaware of God or unrepentant before God.

When we act as if God is not involved in our circumstances, we deny his power in our lives. We go to church, we meet in our small groups, we quote the Bible, but when the rubber hits the road, we know it isn't true and so we handle things according to our human nature. We respond with defensiveness, blame, and self-centeredness.

Anybody can do that. Anybody not connected to Jesus. We are, in that moment, no different from those who appear to have faith but reject its real power (2 Tim. 3:5).

Part of what Jesus is trying to get the disciples to see is that our response in situations of stress and danger is based upon our faith.

Do you believe God is involved in your circumstances or not?

DAY 79

Jesus Allows No Middle Ground

Whoever does not take up their cross
and follow me is not worthy of me.
—Matthew 10:38 (TNIV)

"If we behold Jesus Christ going on before
step by step, we shall not go astray."
—Dietrich Bonhoeffer

Jesus taught that his yoke is easy (Matt. 11:30), but he never said our lives would become easier when we followed him. The truth is, our lives will likely become harder because we're forced to face the harsh reality of life without delusions.

We can't keep pretending everything is okay. We've seen the destructive nature of sin; we understand its real costs; we know we can't wash it all away, only the blood of Jesus can do that.

Where we once could lie or steal or cheat to get what we wanted, now we're in supernatural union with Jesus, and we're required to deal with the reality in our circumstances and relationships, using weapons of Jesus, such as honesty, humility, and grace, and by allowing the Holy Spirit to guide us.

Jesus allows no middle ground.

When we respond from our human nature, instead of submitting to the divine nature working within us, we expose a deep, inner distrust of Jesus. Our actions show we believe him incapable of understanding the stress and danger of life.

On the other hand, when we respond from the truth that we are connected to Jesus, we prove that we believe that he who is within us is greater than he who is in the world (1 John 4:4).

The call of Christ requires us to rely upon him when we come up against the difficulties of life, particularly when we come up against the enemies of Jesus who seek to persecute us.

Because Christ dwells in us, we know we do not face these trials alone; any attack on us is an attack on Jesus. Our identity is so wrapped up in Jesus that our enemies cannot separate us from him.

DAY 80

Loyal to Your Fears or Loyal to Jesus?

Those who do not take up their cross and follow in my
steps are not fit to be my disciples. Those who try to gain
their own life will lose it; but those who lose their life for
my sake will gain it. Whoever finds their life will lose
it, and whoever loses their life for my sake will find it.

—MATTHEW 10:39 (TNIV)

"The time is short. Eternity is long. It is
the time of decision . . . The final decision
must be made while we are still on earth."

—DIETRICH BONHOEFFER

Will we be loyal to our fears or loyal to Jesus?

Jesus says we should know this: if we fear we will lose out on life by following him, the truth is we will lose it all anyway, and at the same time, we will lose out on the real life we're searching for.

On the other hand, if we abandon our fears and follow him, he will lead us into the kingdom of heaven, where we will find the life we always hoped for.

It's a very practical decision unless you're trapped in the kind of fallen thinking that tells us disposable things and temporary relationships are the end all and be all of the universe.

When someone argues that following Jesus is impractical, it shows they do not have a clue about the kingdom of heaven. "The Message that points to Christ on the Cross seems like sheer silliness to those hell-bent on destruction, but for those on the way of salvation it makes perfect sense," says the Apostle Paul (1 Cor. 1:18 MSG).

When we suggest the commands of Jesus are impractical or unrealistic, we show our own ignorance about the kingdom of heaven

And so Jesus comes with his eye on the final judgment. With his cross, Jesus brings peace, notes Bonhoeffer, but "the cross is the sword God wields on earth." The word of God is "sharp as a surgeon's scalpel, cutting through everything, whether doubt or defense, laying us open to listen and obey" (Heb. 4:12 MSG). Jesus slices across our loyalties, demanding that we choose him as our priority.

From now on, any of our relationships must be brought to the feet of Jesus. We can only relate to them in this way, subjugating even our families to the reality of Jesus in our lives.

Jesus will not share his prominence in your life with anyone else. Knowing this, what relationships in your life need to change?

DAY 81
Love Sticks to Its Mission

A new command I give you: Love one another.

—JOHN 13:34A (TNIV)

"The love of Jesus is something very
different from our own zeal and enthusiasms
because it adheres to its mission."

—DIETRICH BONHOEFFER

Jesus commands us to love even the unlovable. In fact,
that is what makes Christian community unique.

He directs us to love one another in the same way that
he has loved us. Quite a tall order, wouldn't you say? He
issues a command that we be to one another what he is
to us. We are directed by his orders to get in step with his
perfect love that is already present within us.

We are to let his love shape our lives; otherwise, we will
not only be distracted from our mission, we'll struggle
to grow up in Christ. We'll become dissatisfied and
discontented because we're stuck in a place of perpet-
ual immaturity.

Love, the kind Jesus calls us to provide, pushes us to
grow up as we get out of ourselves and into the lives

of others. It forces us out of our fantasies, where other people are always accommodating us and doing what we want them to do.

And that is when we begin to learn to really love others in the way that he loves us. We learn to love others, regardless of performance or appearance.

How do you want to be loved? How can you love others in the same way?

DAY 82

Jesus Must Suffer and Be Rejected

*Peter took him aside and began to rebuke him. "Never,
Lord!" he said. "This shall never happen to you!" Jesus
turned and said to Peter, "Get behind me, Satan! You
are a stumbling block to me; you do not have in mind
the concerns of God, but merely human concerns."*

—MATTHEW 16:22–23 (TNIV)

"Suffering and rejection are laid upon Jesus as a
divine necessity, and every attempt to prevent
it is the work of the devil, especially when it
comes from his own disciples; for it is in fact an
attempt to prevent Christ from being Christ."

—DIETRICH BONHOEFFER

We come to the point when we respond to the call of Jesus but then, like Peter, our discipleship breaks down when we find ourselves in disagreement with Jesus. We retreat from the reality back into the shadows of our finite thinking. In Peter's case, Jesus explained he must suffer and be rejected, but this didn't match Peter's image of what the Messiah should be.

Peter stopped thinking like someone who lives in the kingdom of heaven and, ignoring the Father's wisdom, insisted on the right to decide, not only for himself but also for Jesus.

The strong rebuke from Jesus came because Peter's insistence was nothing short of an assault on God's sovereignty. As Bonhoeffer notes, suffering and rejection are "laid upon Jesus as a divine necessity and every attempt to prevent it is the work of the devil, especially when it comes from his own disciples; for it is in fact an attempt to prevent Christ from being Christ."

Our sin costs Jesus and, in light of his suffering, we can no longer pretend that grace is cheap. Jesus must not only suffer; he must also be rejected. Otherwise, Bonhoeffer says, a suffering Messiah may appear as something heroic and "all the sympathy and admiration of the world might have been focused on his passion."

But Jesus is a rejected Messiah and that "robs the passion of its halo of glory." He dies without honor, despised and rejected of men.

How has your fear of rejection kept you from a more mature faith?

DAY 83

Kingdom Hearts, Kingdom Thinking

Then he turned toward the woman and said to Simon, "Do you see this woman? I came into your house. You did not give me any water for my feet, but she wet my feet with her tears and wiped them with her hair."

—LUKE 7:44 (TNIV)

"As if their own needs and their own distress were not enough, they take upon themselves the distress and humiliation and sin of others."

—DIETRICH BONHOEFFER

Jesus pushes the disciples toward kingdom thinking, where cruel words are like instruments of murder, verbal shotgun blasts into the faces of our adversaries.

We use ethnic, gender, and sexual slurs to dehumanize those who oppose us, who are different from us, who don't agree with us, who are a danger to us. They allow us to feel superior, when we are no different from them. We are all created in the image of God; we are all loved equally by Jesus.

We live in a fallen world—Jesus is well aware of that—and so it would be naive to assume we will not run up against real evil that is out to destroy us, but the point is that even those engaged in evil are God's creatures, living with a fallen nature, no different than you and I before Jesus breathed life into our dead spirits.

Kingdom thinking requires that we stop seeing other people, even our enemies, as people we can degrade or judge. Just like us, they are beings in need of God's grace. The sentiment, "There but for the grace of God go I" expresses a legitimate consideration as we interact with friends and foes alike.

As C. S. Lewis explains, we're all eternal beings. The question to be answered is where each of us will spend eternity: in the kingdom of heaven or in dominion of hell.

God's redemptive plan includes the chance for our enemies to come into the kingdom of God under the righteousness of Jesus Christ. They enter in the same way we enter the kingdom of heaven—despite our sins, despite our own weaknesses and imperfections, despite the evil we have committed against others.

No doubt God has already put someone on your mind. What relationship of yours needs to change as you repent of judging that person?

DAY 84

Grace Is a Restaurant

Blessed are those who hunger and thirst
for righteousness, for they will be filled.

—Matthew 5:6 (TNIV)

"I need no longer try to follow Christ, for cheap grace,
the bitterest foe of discipleship, which true discipleship
must loathe and detest, has freed me from that."

—Dietrich Bonhoeffer

Grace is a restaurant where you can eat anything on
the menu for free. The cost for you to dine is hefty,
but your whole bill has been paid for by Jesus.

"You mean, I can eat anything I want here? Then I'll
have a lust burger with a side of lies."

I'm sorry. We don't serve lust burgers or lies here. But
you are welcome to anything on the menu. Everything
here is handmade by the Father and all of it is specifically
designed to keep you healthy.

"I thought you said I could eat anything I wanted if I
came into this grace restaurant?"

You can eat anything you want, but we only serve what is on the menu. If you look, you will see there are thousands of choices we've prepared specifically for your taste buds.

"But not a lust burger? No lie fries? What kind of restaurant are you running here? Don't you want me to be happy, to feel good?"

Happy are those whose greatest desire is to do what God requires; God will satisfy them fully!

"What if I go outside the restaurant, get a lust burger and some lie fries and bring them back in here to eat?"

That would be cheap grace.

DAY 85

The Paradox of Grace

"For this son of mine was dead and is alive again;
he was lost and is found." So they began to celebrate.

—LUKE 15:24 (TNIV)

"The community of the saints is not an 'ideal'
community consisting of perfect and sinless men and
women, where there is no need of further repentance."

—DIETRICH BONHOEFFER

My friend, Paul Carlisle, says the prodigal's father offers a picture of the paradox of grace. The story begins with a self-centered, younger son. He requests his inheritance and then squanders all his father's hard-earned money, ending up working for a pig farmer.

In a state of horrible desperation, he remembers his father and decides to return home as a slave. What was going through his mind as he headed home? Maybe he realized what a failure he was. Or did he think about the money his father gave him that he had foolishly thrown away? Possibly he feared a harsh rejection, one he was sure he deserved.

Whatever he thought, he was not prepared for his father's response!

Imagine: He sees his father's house in the distance as he shamefully shuffles home. Then he sees an unidentifiable person running toward him. Then, he recognizes his father and prepares himself for the worst.

Carlisle suggests the prodigal was probably bewildered by his father's loving embrace. The father's love faces off against the son's self-degradation. The father is overjoyed at the son's return. This is too much for the son. He only hopes for a job as a slave, and yet he is treated as a son despite all his filthiness.

Rather than being embarrassed by the wayward son, the father responds with merriment. The father's response to a rebellious son is a beautiful picture of transforming grace.

Each of us has had our prodigal experiences. Prodigal behavior is common because our heart's default setting is "trust yourself at all costs." Self-trust is rooted in the belief that we will be more gracious to ourselves than God will. Who are we kidding, anyway?

Ask Jesus to personally tutor you in Grace 101. As you receive his grace, turn to others and recklessly heap his grace upon them.

DAY 86

The Community Called Heaven

With all wisdom and understanding, he made known
to us the mystery of his will according to his good
pleasure, which he purposed in Christ, to be put into
effect when the times reach their fulfillment—to bring
unity to all things in heaven and on earth under Christ.

—EPHESIANS 1:8B–10 (TNIV)

"It is a community of men and women who
have genuinely encountered the precious grace
of God, and who walk worthily of the gospel
by not casting that grace recklessly away."

—DIETRICH BONHOEFFER

If the kingdom of heaven is about celebrating the
God who is perfect life and perfect love, where each
Christian will be fulfilled to the highest order, then our
community as Christians here on earth is about celebrating the God-life we share in common, using the strength
of God that is at work in us to see everyone of our Christ-community mature in Christ (Col. 1:28–29).

For the moment, that means we are in the midst of
some rather serious on-the-job-training. God is making

use of all things—pain and suffering, joy and comfort, opposition and cooperation—to reproduce and express the fullness of Christ in us. All that touches us is designed to de-center us from our self-for-self mentality in order to be re-centered in God's self-for-others nature.

Jesus came and demonstrated that only sacrificial love can overcome Satan, sin, the world, the flesh, and death. Each and every believer now has the opportunity to be an "overcomer."

When, in faith, we allow the sacrificial love of Christ to reign and to rule and get the final word in all our relationships, we learn to love as Christ loves and we are perfected—made ready to reign with him by the rule of love through all eternity.

When we love with the love of Jesus, we succeed at everything. Other people can stop us from doing many things, but they cannot stop us from loving them. Only we can stop that love from flowing through us by giving priority to our own self-interest, or by clinging to such things as bitterness, pride, and busyness.

Jesus enlarges our capacity to know and express the nature of God who is love. This is what de-centers us and moves us into the spacious and unlimited other-centeredness of God.

And it is only in the rare air of love that genuine community can breathe.

DAY 87

The Opposite of Fear Is Faith

We should go up and take possession
of the land, for we can certainly do it.

—NUMBERS 13:30B

"If we fall into the hands of men, and meet suffering
and death from their violence, we are none the
less certain that everything comes from God."

—DIETRICH BONHOEFFER

When the Israelites first approached the borders of Canaan, Moses sent scouts into the Promised Land to assess the situation. Ten of the scouts came back with reports that focused on the giants in the land, men so big and powerful the scouts feared they could not be defeated.

However, two of the scouts focused on the promise from God that he would hand the land over to the Israelites. One of those scouts, Caleb, silenced the others when he said, "We should go up and take possession of the land, for we can certainly do it" (Num. 13:30).

Caleb trusted God instead of trusting his own fear. The opposite of fear is faith, the belief that Jesus is capable of handling anything we may face in life. But operating out of faith means we must rely on Jesus, remaining dependent on him to see us through any issue.

He brings us to a choice: Will we trust God or will we trust our own fears?

The Bible says, "The fear of the Lord is the beginning of wisdom" (Prov. 9:10a). In other words, we hold God in reverence, recognizing his sovereignty, authority, and omnipotence—his ability to protect us in any situation. And we reach that level of trust by knowing the Father and understanding his character: "[K]nowledge of the Holy One is understanding" (Prov. 9:10b).

We know and understand the Father by following Jesus. "To see me is to see the Father," says Jesus. "Don't you believe that I am in the Father and the Father is in me? The words that I speak to you aren't mere words. I don't just make them up on my own. The Father who resides in me crafts each word into a divine act" (John 14:9b–10 MSG).

Your fear simply reveals a place where you aren't yet trusting in Jesus. Don't stay stuck in your fear, and don't receive condemnation for your lack of faith. Jesus wants to move you past that into a place where your fears are replaced by faith. Follow him and learn to trust.

DAY 88

'So Do Not Be Afraid of People'

So do not be afraid of them.

—MATTHEW 10:26A (TNIV)

"Those who are still afraid of men have
no fear of God, and those who have fear
of God have ceased to be afraid of men."

—DIETRICH BONHOEFFER

When we fear what other people may think, say, or do, we let them steal the freedom we have in Jesus. They put us back under the law and under the fear of judgment—and that means we live in the mythology that they have a greater power over our lives than God, the Creator and Master of the Universe.

Instead, we need to get our thinking right. God is bigger than anyone or anything. God is in control at all times. Instead of fearing men, who at best can kill us, we should instead fear God, who has the authority to decide where we will spend eternity. Stop seeing simply the shadows that are right in front of you and start seeing things from the reality of life in the kingdom of heaven.

The struggle is that we, both passively and aggressively, insist that fear set the agenda. And then fear pushes us into a life based on self-interest. We make choices based on our fears and not on our faith in God. In fear, we look out for ourselves and that means we act exactly like those who have no faith. We live faithlessly even as we claim to worship a sovereign, omnipotent God who created and keeps the universe, an almighty being who keeps his promises.

We must face the question, "Do I believe God keeps his promises or not?" How will your daily life change if the answer is "yes"?

Faith Should Shape Our Lives

Are not two sparrows sold for a penny? Yet not one of them will fall to the ground outside your Father's care. And even the very hairs of your head are all numbered. So don't be afraid; you are worth more than many sparrows.

—MATTHEW 10:29-31 (TNIV)

"The same God who sees no sparrow fall to the ground without his knowledge and will, allows nothing to happen, except it be good and profitable for his children and the cause for which they stand. We are in God's hands. Therefore, 'Fear not.'"

—DIETRICH BONHOEFFER

Jesus says fear should no longer shape our lives. It keeps us out of step with him, and he will stop at nothing, including a bloody cross, to eliminate fear from our lives. He commands that we begin making decisions in faith and not in fear.

In Jesus, we find an uncommon safety that promises God is present even when we face our greatest fears. The choice is, will we believe God when he says, "For I know the plans I have for you . . . plans to prosper you and not to harm you, plans to give you hope and a future" (Jer. 29:11)? Within this promise is an acknowledgement from God that we may, for a time, view his plans as disastrous, perhaps even evil, yet we are still told, "Fear not!"

If God knows when a sparrow falls and you are worth more than the sparrow, don't you think the Father will take care of you? Jesus is teaching us kingdom thinking. This is the way our minds were created to think before the devil whispered doubt and distrust into the neural network of our brains. Jesus, again, pushes us to a choice: will we trust our fears or will we trust the word of God?

The point is, we are in God's hands and so what we fear can never be viewed as separate from that truth. Fear not; God is taking care of you. Jesus is not suggesting we will no longer face terrible situations once we stop being afraid. Jesus is not naive about the reality of evil in this world; the men who crucified Jesus were an incarnation of that evil. Yet God used even that for his own great purposes.

All things—even the things we fear—work together for the good of those who love God and are called by Jesus to his purposes. Think of the worst thing anyone can do to you and think about how God can redeem that evil in some way.

How would your perspective change if you trusted that God is taking all the bad things in your life and re-creating them to bring good into your life?

DAY 90

If You Knew the Generosity of God

*Jesus answered, "If you knew the generosity of
God and who I am, you would be asking me for a
drink, and I would give you fresh, living water."*

JOHN 4:10 (MSG)

"We pay no attention to our own lives or the new
image which we bear, for then we should at once
have forfeited it, since it is only to serve as a mirror
for the image of Christ on whom our gaze is fixed."

—DIETRICH BONHOEFFER

Grace allows people to make choices and assumes
they'll make the best choice. Grace is free and flowing and unencumbered by guilt or shame or fear, for true
grace says, "I know all about you, and I still love you with a
godly acceptance."

We see this in John 4, when Jesus meets the woman at
the well. When she offers to give him a drink, he says, "If
you knew the generosity of God and who I am, you would
be asking me for a drink, and I would give you fresh living
water" (4:10 MSG).

Note that he talks about how gracious God can be. Yet most of us, if we were honest, function as if God were stingy with his grace. We fear his punishment, in the sense that we think he's the high school principal walking the halls, taking down names. Who did what and who's to blame?

But God already knows who did what and who's to blame, and he still loves us anyway. His interest is in redeeming us, not in keeping us on the hook for our sins.

Unfortunately, many of us Christians live our lives as if we're still on the hook, and as if we have to keep everyone else on the hook. We use weapons of the flesh—the sarcastic comment, the angry stare—all designed to get people to straighten up and live right.

In contrast, when the woman at the well goes back to her village, she says, "Come see a man . . . who knows me inside and out" (John 4:29 MSG). Nothing is hidden from him, and yet he communicates with her in such a fashion that she leaves the well feeling loved and accepted.

That's grace.

CONCLUSION

The Journey Begins with Jesus

One day the people couldn't find Jesus, so they went looking for him. When they found him, he was all the way on the other side of the Sea of Galilee, complexly opposite from where they originally thought he would be (John 6:22-70).

"How long have you been here?" they asked.

Jesus didn't answer their specific question; instead, he spoke the truth in love, telling them that the only reason they followed him was because he'd given them free bread.

"You worked hard trying to find me, so you could get more bread," he said, in a sense. "Why work so hard for something that's so temporary? Put your efforts into things eternal."

The people asked, "We want to perform God's works too. What should we do?"

Jesus answered, "This is the only work God wants from you: Believe in the one he has sent" (based on John 6:28-29 NLT).

Their search for Jesus had brought them to the opposite side of the lake from where they thought he would be and now he wanted them to start thinking opposite of their human nature, to stop thinking like mere mortals and start listening for the thoughts of God. He wanted them to enter into kingdom thinking and abandon their fallen thinking.

Jesus calls us to the same thing today. He wants us to enter into kingdom thinking and abandon our fallen thinking. We seek Jesus, thinking we know where we will find him—in religious traditions, in burdensome rules, in good behavior, in pious posturing; in feel-good fantasies that lead to cheap grace.

We ask, "What can we do in order to do what God wants us to do?" And Jesus says it's not about trying harder, but trusting more. What God wants you to do is obediently believe in the one he sent. Seek him and his righteousness and everything else will be provided.

Again, Jesus pushes to make a choice: will we keep trying to find that one thing we must do, or will we simply trust Jesus and believe what he says?

Instead of exhausting ourselves trying to please God, Jesus says we will please God when we put our efforts into believing the One sent by God, Jesus, the Father's own Son. We're to make every effort to enter the rest of God, not to earn the favor of God (Heb. 4:1-14).

Instead of trying harder, Jesus tells us to trust more.

In Jesus, the Father's only Son, the fullness of divine nature lives and, through Christ, we have been given full life in union with him (Col. 2:9-10). In other words, we are complete in Christ. At the moment of conversion, we are given everything we need to succeed at the abundant life, everything we need to live a life of extraordinary quality, one that carries significance beyond ourselves.

The character of Christ is already at work in us; the mind of Christ is already available to us. We are "more than conquerors through him who loved us" (Rom. 8:37 NIV). We now "come from God and belong to God" and "the Spirit in [us] is far stronger than anything in the world" (1 John 4:4 MSG).

There is nothing we can do to add to what God has already done. Nothing.

Our job is to trust and rest in the truth that our safety and security is in Jesus. The full and complete life of Christ that is already in us will emerge, not because we try harder, but because we obediently trust the Word of God.

"My counsel for you is simple and straightforward: Just go ahead with what you've been given," says Paul. "You received Christ Jesus, the Master; now live him. You're deeply rooted in him. You're well constructed upon him. You know your way around the faith. Now do what you've been taught. School's out; quit studying the subject and start living it! And let your living spill over into thanksgiving" (Col. 2:6-7 MSG).

We trust that Jesus has done the work required for us to boldly approach the throne of God and we rest faithfully in the truth that we can now enter the kingdom of heaven under his banner of righteousness. We believe we are holy, just as our heavenly Father is holy because Jesus is the one who makes us holy (1 Peter 1:16).

It was their refusal to believe this that brought on Paul's rebuke of the Galatians: "Let me ask you this one question: Did you receive the Holy Spirit by obeying the law of Moses? Of course not! You received the Spirit because you believed the message you heard about Christ. How foolish can you be? After starting your Christian lives in the Spirit, why are you now trying to become perfect by your own human effort?" (Galatians 3:2-3 NLT

We begin the journey into the kingdom upon our completion in Christ—and that is at the moment of salvation, On the journey Jesus teaches us how to grow-up in Christ so that who we are on the outside matches the life of Christ that flows through our inside.

May you know joy in the journey and may you know with radiant certainty that Jesus, the Word of God, fulfills every one of his promises. He obediently trusted the Father so that you could enter the kingdom of heaven; may you obediently trust Jesus to get you through the narrow gate, where the Father and all of heaven will celebrate your return home (Luke 15:32).

About Dietrich Bonhoeffer

Dietrich Bonheoffer's life was one of risk, where he faced constant choices that required him to take a stand, often putting everything he had—even his life—on the line for what he believed. It's easy to marvel at the way he faced off against Adolf Hitler and the Nazi regime, but in books such as *The Cost of Discipleship* Bonhoeffer taught that a life of such extraordinary risk is the *expectation*, not the exception, for any disciple of Jesus.

A little over a year after Bonhoeffer was ordained as a Lutheran pastor, the Nazi's came to power on January 30, 1933. Bonhoeffer, only twenty-six-years-old, delivered a radio address two days later, where he warned the German people they were being seduced by the Führer and that their worship of him would lead to idolatry. His broadcast was cut off in mid-sentence.

A gifted theologian, Bonhoeffer might have taught in any number of professorships or pastorates, but his opposition to Adolf Hitler closed the door to those opportunities. Instead, he began teaching in less formal settings, such as the unofficial Finkenwalde Seminary.

It was at Finkenwalde that Bonhoeffer began writing *The Cost of Discipleship*, publishing the manuscript in 1937, about the same time the Gestapo shut down the seminary and arrested many of its students.

Although Bonhoeffer was a pacifist, he struggled with the moral obligations a believer faces when confronted with a systemic evil that saturates an entire society and, in this sense, he began fighting for the moral survival of the German people by opposing the Nazi regime. Bonhoeffer was not only aware of various plots against Hitler, he eventually saw the Führer's assassination as a necessary part of restoring the soul of Germany.

After the July 20 plot ("Valkyrie") to assassinate Hitler failed, the Gestapo discovered Bonhoeffer's involvement and his death was ordered by Adolf Hitler. He was executed on April 8, 1945 by hanging at Flossenbürg concentration camp—about three weeks before Hitler committed suicide and the Allies pushed into Berlin.

Bonhoeffer died as he lived, focused exclusively on Christ and humbly submitting to the ultimate cost of discipleship. Offered an opportunity to escape, he declined, not wanting to put his family in danger. He was led to the gallows after concluding a Sunday morning service, saying: "This is the end—for me the beginning of life."

He has become one of the most influential theological voices of the twentieth century and *The Cost of Discipleship* is considered a classic in ecclesiological literature. Many of its concepts are now deeply ingrained in modern Protestant thought and practice.

To read more about Bonhoeffer, see the excellent biography by Eric Metaxas, *Bonhoeffer: Pastor, Martyr, Prophet, Spy* (Thomas Nelson, 2010).

About Jon Walker

JON WALKER has worked closely with Rick Warren for many years, first as a writer/editor at Pastors.com, later as vice president of communications at Purpose Driven Ministries, and then as a pastor at Saddleback Church. He's also served as editor-in-chief of LifeWay's *HomeLife* magazine and founding editor of Rick Warren's *Ministry Toolbox*. His articles have appeared in publications and Web sites around the world. You can learn more about his ministry at www.gracecreates.com.